DEAR CHURCH
WHAT'S
THE POINT?

QUESTIONS
YOUNG CATHOLICS ASK

Raphael Appleby

KEVIN MAYHEW

To Naimh and Fiona

This edition 1989

First published in Great Britain in 1985 by
KEVIN MAYHEW LTD.,
Rattlesden,
Bury St Edmunds, Suffolk IP30 0SZ
Reprinted 1985

©1984 Raphael Appleby and Kevin Mayhew Ltd.

Except for brief quotations embodied in critical articles and reviews, this book may not be reproduced in whole or in part by any means whatever without the prior written permission of the publisher.

ISBN 0 86209 062 8

Typeset by Barry Sarling, Rayleigh, Essex.
Printed in Great Britain at The Bath Press, Avon

Contents

		Page
	Preface	5
I	FEELING USELESS *'I often feel that I'm a pretty useless sort of person...'*	6
II	THE CHURCH *'What actually is the church?'*	16
III	THE POPE, CARDINALS AND BISHOPS *'Do we have to believe everything he says?'*	31
IV	THE MASS *'I find going to mass on Sundays pretty pointless...'*	39
V	CONFESSION *'It's ages since I've been to confession...'*	50
VI	CONFIRMATION *'At eleven years of age could it have been expected to mean much...?'*	57
VII	SEX *'Father, I have a problem...'*	63
VIII	CONTRACEPTION *'Why is the church so out of touch with the rest of the world...?'*	79
IX	PRAYER *'Frequently... it just seems to be a waste of time.'*	87

Preface

This little book is neither a catechism nor a theological treatise. Although only one chapter is presented in conversational style it could most accurately be described as a series of pastoral conversations with young Catholics, most of them sixth formers or students, many of whom find difficulty in sorting out their relationships with the church and with some of her teaching.

Such young people have not inherited the confident, stable, structured church of their parents, characterised by the clear cut answers of the penny catechism. They live in a world which does not know Christianity very well and whose values are almost entirely secular, and are constantly encouraged to strive for more money, more possessions, more pleasures. In this world, to live as a Christian demands more than weekly attendance at mass and a struggle to keep the commandments. It demands more because to live according to the values of the gospel, to seek to serve rather than to use, can only be done with the constant help of God. As one young person put it: 'our need to be with God at all times'.

So often the church seems to them to be out of date, at odds with the world, so many questions need to be discussed. Who to ask? Hence this book. What follows does not provide final answers but is an attempt to start reflections and discussions which could continue when the book has been put down. Nor does it cover all the difficult areas. Most of the material has been written in response to actual questions asked by such young people during the past two years. To have attempted more would have meant too big a book.

I. Feeling Useless

I often feel that I'm a pretty useless sort of person, not much good at anything, weak-willed, and generally rather pathetic. What good can I do?

One of the advantages of being a priest is that people come and talk to you frankly and honestly about themselves, both in confession and outside it. So you learn quite quickly, and with relief, that nearly everyone shares the sort of doubts that you mention. And that's a relief because you feel them too. I find that very many men and women, young and old, feel pretty useless much of the time. Indeed, if they don't, if they feel capable and God's gift to the world, then I tremble for them because it is clear to me that they really have a very limited and ignorant view of themselves and of other people.

First of all, we must learn to understand ourselves as we are, and then to accept that reality and not continually wish we were like someone else. When I was a boy I longed to be bigger, faster, stronger. Since I've grown up I've wanted to be cleverer, more virtuous, less lazy, more eloquent, more influential, and so on. It has taken me a long time to realise that God has made me as I am and that his creation is made up of millions of men and women like me, varied, of course, but essentially similar.

Of course, some people are, or seem to be, much more effective than others, but that means that they have done what they were capable of doing, that's all. As Christians we believe that God has a plan for each one of us; that we were all made by God *on purpose*; that our lives are not the result of random choices, but that God wants us, has chosen us specifically and has a part in his plan for us to play. And that part is specially suited to your character, personality, size, talents, weaknesses, and what-

'We must learn to understand ourselves as we are'

8 Feeling Useless

ever goes to make up you. God doesn't want you any different from what you are. He doesn't make mistakes and he has made you and loves you *as you are*.

It is difficult sometimes, especially when everything seems to be going wrong, to believe that, and one of the hardest lessons for us to learn is that we can't actually do anything of importance in this world without God's help. Indeed, any good we manage to do is simply because we have stopped getting in God's way and have let him do good through us. You know that lovely prayer of St. Francis, 'Make me a channel of your peace', well, I often re-phrase that to read 'Make me a channel of your grace', with the prayer that God will reach people through me and that I won't get in the way, as I continually do if I try to work on my own.

I used to be a school teacher, and I used to look at the bright young things in my classes, pupils who were good at everything, passed all their exams, played in school teams, were liked by their fellows, and I used to worry about them. I worried about them more than about the other pupils who were low down in class, failed their exams, seldom played in teams, and were lacking in confidence. Why? Because the second type of pupil was so much closer to reality. He knew that he was weak and that life would not be easy. He knew that he needed help, both from his friends and from God, and he wasn't too proud to ask for it. But the successful, over-confident boy was much less well equipped to face the inevitable doubts and failures that were to come. And that tended to mean that he either fell at the first real fence, and lost his faith, or went to pieces; or, perhaps more commonly, he constructed a world view with himself at the centre of it, surrounded himself with protective shells, and grew into a reactionary, immovable, sadly ignorant-but-unaware-of-it adult who genuinely believed that he was right and everyone else was wrong. You probably have not yet met such people but they exist in large numbers and they are often not all that old.

Do you remember the story of the rich young man in the gospel? He was just such a person. It is easy to see the confident young man asking Jesus what is necessary to inherit eternal life.

'...pupils who were good at everything'

10 Feeling Useless

As expected, Jesus tells him to keep the commandments, and the young man is able to say smugly that he has kept all the commandments all his life. So he expects a pat on the back from Jesus which will confirm him in his smugness. But what does he get? 'There is one thing you lack. Go and sell everything that you own and give the money to the poor, and you will have treasure in heaven; then come, follow me'. And we are told that he went away sadly, 'for he was a man of great wealth'. Pretty shattering for the poor young man, for all the success he was so proud of counted for nothing in the eyes of Jesus. Perhaps he went away sadly because he decided that Jesus couldn't be the Messiah he was looking for: he simply couldn't cope with the loss of face, the loss of everything that Jesus was asking of him.

That is the first point to understand. Now one of the huge advantages of feeling inadequate and a sense of littleness and failure is that you probably haven't put all your eggs into one basket, whether the basket is filled with success, money, popularity, or what you will. So when Jesus tells you to sell what you have and follow him you find that easier to respond to because you haven't got much to lose. If you read the gospels carefully you find that Jesus was much closer to very ordinary people, men and women who were sinners and knew it, who weren't very special, and yet were drawn to Jesus because he respected them and loved them. Jesus founded his church on people like Peter ('Depart from me, O Lord, for I am a sinful man'); Mary Magdalene ('who had a bad name in the town'); Matthew ('a tax collector'); James and John ('fishermen'): none of them particularly distinguished.

They all *became* saints, but the point is that they started with nothing. And this is the important point: it was only because they had nothing that they were able to listen to Jesus. The rich young man couldn't; the righteous Pharisees couldn't; King Herod couldn't; they were all clogged up with either possessions or their own self-importance and they simply couldn't hear what he was saying to them. Jesus makes the point very clearly when he says 'I came to call, not the just, but sinners'. If we think we are just, we are blind to our own emptiness. It is only when we know that we are sinners, weak, selfish, mean, that we understand our own importance and can realise that it is only by getting close to God that we can achieve anything.

So the first lesson for all of us is that, yes, we are sinners, but thank God that we are! For the second lesson is that it is as sinners that God loves us, *as we are here and now*, not as we dream of being one day. And if God loves you as you are, must you not accept and love yourself too? If Jesus considers that you are worth living and dying for should you not feel loved and wanted by him?

St. Thérèse of Lisieux used to thank God for her littleness and lack of importance. She understood the values of the gospel, how God chooses the weak to confound the strong. She used to ask Jesus to let her snuggle up to him so that she could feel utterly safe in his arms.

Now I want to say something about the vocation of the lay man and woman in the church. Often we feel that there is a clear enough vocation for the priest or the sister, and indeed for the married couple. But what about the unmarried, the ordinary boy and girl, young man and young woman? Are they still marking time, preparing for an unknown future, or what?

The Second Vatican Council has a lot to say about this. It reminds us that when we are baptised we are baptised into the life, death and resurrection of Jesus. That may sound heavily theoretical but it isn't so. It means, quite simply, that we share the life of Jesus, that once baptised we are one with him. (Perhaps the nearest human example is when we recognise the married couple as becoming one with each other). Jesus comes and makes his dwelling place within us; we share his life, and are no longer alone for we have the life of Jesus intimately bound up with our own. St. Paul puts it dramatically: 'I live now, not I; for Christ lives in me'. We are part of the Body of Christ.

This life begins at baptism, although it may not be until we have grown up a little that we can begin to understand what it means. For its full meaning is quite remarkable. If we truly share the life, death and resurrection of Jesus, then we share everything that belongs to him. His love, his strength, his joy belongs to us. And so does his mission. His mission, for which he was sent by his Father, to bring the world to God, to proclaim the kingdom of God in this world. St. Peter puts it very clearly: you are 'the holy priesthood that offers the spiritual sacrifices which Jesus Christ has made acceptable to God'.

There is, of course, a special vocation to the ordained priesthood and that vocation is explained by the Council as follows: 'The clergy are to minister to the Christian people so that their union with Christ will be strong and that they may exercise their calling in the world'. *All* Christians through baptism share in the priesthood of Christ. *Some* are called to minister to the rest, to help them fulfil their vocation which is to offer spiritual sacrifices to God. So what does Christ's priesthood really mean? Well, a priest is one who is empowered to offer sacrifices to God. And that means that he or she has the power to make the offerings holy because unless the offering is holy it cannot be acceptable to God.

Jesus offered himself, and because he was God his offering was perfect and so totally acceptable to God. Because God has become man through Jesus he wants to offer the whole world to God, every man and woman who has ever lived, the whole of creation. Now man has sinned so that he is unacceptable to God. But Jesus has identified himself with man so that *with Jesus* we are acceptable to God. Is that clear? Men and women, united with Christ, become perfect and acceptable to God. Christ's job as priest was to make us holy and so acceptable to God.

By ourselves we are sinful and imperfect and so cannot live with God in heaven, but with Jesus we can. And because we share Christ's priesthood we are 'empowered to present ourselves as a living sacrifice, holy and pleasing to God' (Vat. 2). In other words we are empowered to make the world holy, and that is Christ's mission, and our mission, and the mission of the church to the world: to make it holy for God; to save the world.

And we do that by doing all that we do 'in the Spirit'. By bearing hardships 'patiently'. By living 'with generous hearts'. The Council is very explicit about all this. It says: 'For all their works, prayers and apostolic endeavours, their ordinary married and family life, their daily occupations, their physical and mental relaxation, *if carried out in the Spirit*, and even the hardships of life, *if patiently borne*—all these become "spiritual sacrifices to God through Jesus Christ".

What this means is that everything we do has value in the eyes of God if we do it generously, in harmony with God's will. Even the simple actions of every day—getting up, eating meals, working, playing, reading—all have their place. And the hardships, and that includes our inadequacies, failures, loneliness, personal weaknesses, 'if patiently borne', become part of this offering of our lives to God through and with Jesus which is holy and acceptable to him. This means that the trivia of my very unimportant daily life can be turned into something important which make not only me but the whole world holy.

And that is the truth of it. A very good description of it can be found in the life of St. Thérèse of Lisieux, what she called her 'little way'. The important thing is doing it in the Spirit, being generous in the way we approach each person, accepting the hurts and sufferings, wanting to do God's will rather than our own. And that is not always easy, but with God's help it is always possible.

You may well ask whether we shouldn't be doing something more directly to help those who are hungry or are suffering in some way, but I think the truth of it is that if you grow close to God in prayer, if you try to do each day what you believe he wants you to do, if you really learn to listen to the people around you and to look at your life and other people's lives through the eyes of faith, then you will almost certainly find that you are drawn irresistibly to try to help in whatever way you can. You may *feel* useless, and indeed you are, *on your own*, but with the love and the power of Christ in your heart he can do a lot through you.

God wants you to use the gifts he has given you. Maybe you can't do much. But you can pray; you can try to live your daily life generously; you can listen to people who want to talk. You may well find if you keep your eyes and ears open that there are little things you can do to help: perhaps a spot of hospital or old people's home visiting; possibly some assistance is needed by a local charity, delivering letters or selling flags. These are little beginnings: some may lead to bigger things. And to them all you can bring some love and commitment, a smile and some hopefulness. These things matter enormously.

Furthermore, you can be loyal to your friends; you can deepen your love and your belonging to your family and friends; you can really try to offer yourself and all you do to God in the mass. You can welcome, accept and support people.

You need to remember that the strength and the love that will make this possible for you comes from Jesus who lives in your heart. To draw upon that love it is necessary to get close to him and keep ever growing closer. How? Mainly by prayer, but also by reading the Bible and using the sacraments. Not only holy communion but also confession.

If you want to be able to share in God's plan for the world, to do with your life what he wants you to do, then you will want to give some time to making this journey with God. That does mean giving time, preferably each day, to being alone with God. It means trying to listen to him in your heart, through the scriptures, through the needs and hopes of the people around you.

It often helps to gather a few friends together so that you can help one another, both to be persevering and generous in your prayers and your study, and to support and encourage each other daily. Just one like-minded friend makes a big difference. There may be some other young people in your parish or in your chaplaincy who would really like to join you. A Young Christian Workers group, or a Young Christian Students group can be an excellent way to start. Or form your own group. Don't be discouraged. Remember the old Chinese proverb: 'a journey of a thousand miles starts with a single step'.

'Form your own group'

II. The Church

I think of rows and rows of regally seated bishops with the Pope at their head...of people...of a building...of rules and regulations. What actually is the church?

We ought to begin with the gospels and see what they have to tell us. For we know that the first Christians told the people about Jesus Christ, who he was and how he had risen from the dead. They asked for belief in him, baptised their converts, and encouraged them to live a life in accordance with that belief. So what does Jesus tell us in the gospels? 'He who believes has eternal life... Love one another even as I have loved you'. Jesus underlines the ancient law of the Jews: 'You must love the Lord your God with your whole heart, and your whole soul and with your whole strength, and your neighbour as yourself'. And who is my neighbour? Well, you will be familiar with the story of the good Samaritan and with the story of the judgement of the sheep and the goats: 'If you did it to the least of these my little ones you did it unto me'.

Jesus came to offer men and women a share in his life of love with God. Put like that it may sound rather bald, the sort of religious jargon that we are always hearing and from which we so often switch off. So let's look at it from a different angle.

Consider your ambitions. They may be concerned with the immediate future, passing 'A' levels, getting that degree safely, sorting out a job or career; or they may be concerned with getting married, or something to do with the current boy friend or girl friend; or they may be more a question of being liked or respected or even just accepted by your peers. There are times in your life when questions of self-identity loom large: perhaps when running into difficulties at home, clashes with parents

'Consider your ambitions'

over behaviour or status, or when finding yourself away from home for the first time, wondering just where you belong and who cares anyway. At such moments the most important questions concern being accepted for what you are, being loved just for being yourself, regardless of success or failure. Do you belong?

Sometimes you may feel: I don't want to belong to anyone; I cherish independence; I want to be free; I resent being tied down by family obligations. But if I don't belong to anyone at all, just exactly who am I? There are the occasional self-sufficient hermits but even they go mad if they don't belong to God. Is it possible to be fully happy and complete as a person without belonging to anyone else at all, with no responsibilities for anyone else, and with no-one belonging to me? It's worth thinking about because I suggest that it is only through the people we belong to that we truly begin to discover ourselves. Through their eyes we find out who we are and that we are valued and loved. I often notice in a young couple about to get married the joyful condition that is best described as 'blooming'. Why? Because each knows that they are loved and so feels

'Sometimes you may feel: I don't want to belong to anyone'

confident and happy, quite sure about self-identity and value and so able to face the world and anything that comes along.

Most people know that, whatever the arguments and difficulties that crop up from time to time, they belong to their families. They will always be welcome there; they don't have to justify their right to be there. Most parents are committed to their children, whatever the children may get up to. And the insecurity of children without such parents is only too apparent. So, perhaps grudgingly at times, most of us would admit to belonging to our families. Do we belong to anyone else? Does anyone else belong to us?

A student in her first term at college may well wonder whether she belongs anywhere when she comes back to her empty, lonely room and wonders how to fill in the evening. She may long for a friend, for a group where she will be welcomed, where she will know that she belongs. Let's think again about what Jesus says in the gospels. Doesn't love have a lot to do with belonging, with accepting people, being responsible for them, caring for them? We talk about love in lots of different ways and it may have lots of different meanings, but being committed to someone else is a meaning to which nearly everyone can respond: wanting what is best for the other person, which involves a commitment. Jesus told us to love one another 'as I have loved you'. As St. Paul makes clear, Jesus willingly gave up his divinity, *emptied himself*, and became a man. Why? Not just to show us how to love but to enable us to love. To make it possible for us to belong to him and to one another. If you read the gospels carefully you will find Jesus slowly telling us about his life, his relationship with the Father: 'the Father and I are one...if you have seen me you have seen the Father', and you will perhaps begin to understand that he is talking about love, that total belonging and acceptance of one another.

Jesus says much, too, of what it means in practice to love one another: not to judge, to forgive, to walk another mile with, to share one's cloak, to heal, to spend time with; and, finally, 'there is no greater love than that a man lay down his life for his friends', and so he dies on the cross. And his last message?

'I call you friends...the Father and I will come and make our dwelling place within you...I pray that they will be one even as you and I are one'.

So Jesus is talking about belonging. Telling us that we belong to him and he to us, and that to belong we must love one another and let ourselves be loved. And all that is necessary is that we believe Jesus and let his love work in us so that we can love one another. On that is based the whole of Christianity, the whole of the church.

But Jesus gave his disciples two explicit commands. He told them to baptise in his name and to share the bread and the wine of the eucharist: 'do this in memory of me'. These are visible signs of belonging to Jesus. People who have been baptised belong to a visible community of Christians and the regular, strengthening sign of their belonging to God and each other is their sharing of the eucharist.

There is, in practice, what we may call both a visible and an invisible church. The *visible* church is the community of those who have been baptised and who acknowledge membership of the church. Everyone who bases his life on love is part of the *invisible* church. He may belong to another Christian church, or to a non-Christian religion, or may not be a believer at all; but such people are living the command of Christ to love one another and it is Christ himself in the world who makes such love possible. Wherever we find love we find Christ even if he is not explicitly recognised and may even be denied. And the opposite is also true. Wherever love is lacking, there Christ is lacking too, and may even be being blasphemed if what is done is done in the name of Christ and yet is characterised by selfishness, injustice and rejection, rather than by love, justice and acceptance.

For Jesus has redeemed the whole world. By becoming one with us he has joined himself to all men and women in an indissoluble bond of love, and his Spirit is at work in the world even where it is not recognised as such. Hence, we can find goodness, generosity and holiness in the most unexpected places.

It is the word of God that matters, the word that came

through Jesus into this world and works now and always in our hearts and the hearts of all men and women everywhere, urging us to *act justly, love tenderly and walk humbly with our God.* The Spirit works through the consciences of men and women, guiding them according to their lights, and he is not bound by the limits of the visible church. Indeed, we can see at times, and sadly, how the visible church hides rather than reveals the love of God for mankind. Where there is hatred, or bigotry, or prejudice, or selfishness, or racism, or sexism, or narrow mindedness, or rejection, or injustice, or exclusiveness, or so much else, then the visible church is hiding God. And if you look at the history of Christianity since the time of Christ you will find many examples of the church hiding rather than revealing the love of God.

Aristides, a non-Christian, defended the Christians before the emperor Hadrian, in the second century A.D., in the following words:

> Christians love one another. They never fail to help widows; they save orphans from those who would hurt them. If a man has something, he gives freely to the man who has nothing. If they see a stranger, Christians take him home and are

'The visible church hides rather than reveals the love of God for mankind'

happy, as though he were a real brother. They don't consider themselves brothers in the usual sense, but brothers instead through the Spirit, in God. And if they hear that one of them is in gaol, or persecuted for professing the name of their redeemer, they all give him what he needs... This is really a new kind of person. There is something divine in them.*

We may find in these words a challenge to the visible church as it is often seen to-day, when clericalism, too much interest in position, wealth, rubrics and comfortable living seem to characterise an uncomfortable amount of our Western Christianity.

This may seem to suggest that the visible church is not all that necessary, but it isn't as simple as that, for Jesus started a visible community of believers. In reply to Peter's declaration of faith: 'You are the Christ...the Son of the living God', Jesus said: 'You are Peter and on this rock I will build my Church'. The word for 'church' in Greek means 'an assembly called together', a community of those who believe. He told them to baptise all nations, to share his body and blood in the eucharist, and to teach, not really possible without some form of visible church. And as the number of Christians grew in the early years it became inevitable that some form of organisation would be needed to ensure that the gospel of Jesus would be truly preached and taught. The modern confusing growth of sects, both Christian and pseudo-Christian, may show us how difficult it is to understand the gospel without some properly organised church with a true authority to preach and teach. But we should not forget that the visible church is essentially the community of the baptised: those who have accepted Jesus Christ as the son of God and the redeemer of all men and women, who profess that belief in their regular sharing of the eucharist and in the lives they try to lead. And while recognising that community of all the baptised, the Catholic church believes that she has inherited the authority of Christ to teach all nations.

In 1963 Pope John XXIII summoned a council of all the bishops of the Catholic church. From quite an early date in the

*Quoted in *The Eucharist and Human Liberation* by Tissa Balasuriya (SCM Press).

'In 1963 Pope John XXIII summoned a council'

history of Christianity bishops were established as leaders of the local churches and that practice has continued ever since. The bishop is the presider over the eucharist and the leader of the Christian community. He has the responsibility of ensuring that the apostolic witness to the resurrection continues, and that whoever teaches Christianity in his diocese teaches it faithfully in accordance with the scriptures themselves and the tradition of the church. Hence bishops are often called successors of the Apostles.

So Pope John called together about 2,500 such bishops from all over the world for what came to be called a pastoral council, known as the Second Vatican Council. The object of the Council was to re-examine the basic belief and teaching and practice of the Catholic church in the light of twentieth century problems to ensure that the church was not obscuring the faith through obsolete style, language or method. One of the first achievements of the Council was the reform of the liturgy, including the mass, and the introduction of local languages instead of the universal use of Latin. But the Council will probably be best remembered for its document on the church, called *Lumen Gentium*. That document tried to examine what the church is and what is its function.

It would be impossible in this short account to do justice to *Lumen Gentium*. Let it suffice to say that the Council recognised the existence of both the visible and the invisible churches, and when describing the nature of the visible church found it necessary to look at it from several points of view, offering various descriptive models of the church, no one of which could be considered adequate on its own, but all of which are necessary for a full understanding of the church.

One such model is of the church as the *people of God*. This means the community of all those who have been baptised, whether in infancy or adulthood. This is really the visible church, those who have heard and accepted in at least some measure the word of God, who are known to be Christians, who try to live their lives to a greater or less degree in accordance with what they believe to be the will of God. This community of the baptised includes all the different Christian denominations that accept baptism, and it is the essential ingredient of being a member of the visible church of God. Through baptism we share in the life, death and resurrection of Jesus. Jesus came on earth that we might be able to share his life, become one with him, be united with him in his life, death and resurrection; baptism is the visible sign of this unity. The pouring of the water signifies dying to the world of sin and evil and rising with Christ to the life of holiness and generosity and love.

There is a further significance in baptism. After his resurrection Jesus returned to his Father but told us through the gospels that he would remain in this world: 'the Father and I will come and make our dwelling place within you'; and again: 'you are the temples of the Holy Spirit', as St. Paul tells us. So Jesus lives in us in the world. If the world is to find Christ where must it look? At the people of God, the people chosen and entrusted by God with his presence in the world.

The Council stresses this understanding when it calls the church also the *Sacrament of Christ's presence* in the world. A sacrament is something visible, tangible, that expresses a reality that is invisible and spiritual. The church, the people of God, is a visible community; it expresses an invisible reality, the presence of Christ in the world. It is the ever living sign of hope to all the world in its belief that God lives and that his word is ever active in our lives and that we are called to share his destiny.

The Council raised further questions. How did Jesus see himself? If the church is to be a visible sign of Christ's presence in the world, what sort of a sign should it be? Well, we don't have to look very far for an answer: 'the Son of Man came not to be served but to serve'. St. John recounts, in his story of the Last Supper, how Jesus knelt down and washed the feet of his disciples. Peter protested. Why? Because he knew well that such menial tasks were properly done by slaves. But Jesus insisted. And when he had finished he said to them quite plainly that he, whom they rightly called Lord and Master, had performed the most humble task for each of them. 'Go, and do likewise', he told them.

In the prophecy of Isaiah there is a famous passage concerning the suffering servant. Part of it goes like this:

> Without beauty, without majesty we saw him,
> no looks to attract our eyes;
> a thing despised and rejected by men,
> a man of sorrows and familiar with suffering...
>
> And yet ours were the sufferings he bore,
> ours the sorrows he carried...
>
> On him lies a punishment that brings us peace,
> and through his wounds we are healed...
>
> By his sufferings shall my servant justify many,
> taking their faults on himself.

Christians have always recognised that as a portrait of Jesus. When Jesus started his public ministry St. Luke tells us that he went into the synagogue and read the following passage from Isaiah:

> The spirit of the Lord
> has been given to me,
> for he has anointed me.
> He has sent me to bring
> the good news to the poor,
> to proclaim liberty to captives
> and to the blind new sight,
> to set the downtrodden free,
> to proclaim the Lord's year of favour.

And then he told them: 'This text is being fulfilled to-day even as you listen'.

Jesus came to set men and women free from all that holds them captive. If the church is to be true to herself, to be Christ in the world, then she has a mission to set people free. To set them free from what? Here we touch the very heart of the church's mission. What do we need to be set free from? From poverty, oppression, hunger—yes. But perhaps more importantly from whatever stops us from belonging to one another, whether it be the fear of other people's opinions, or public

The Church 27

pressure to conform to standards which are not Christian: from anything that stops us from loving each other as Jesus commanded us to do.

What is it that makes us jealous, eager to do each other down; callous in regard to the suffering of others; full of greed and lust, idleness and selfishness? Why is it that one third of the world is rich and well fed and two thirds are poor and hungry? Perhaps it is because we are fearful of one another, worried about what other people think of us, under pressure to conform to the world's standards, greedy for success and recognition; and slaves, too, of our own passions and needs.

Where are men and women going to find the courage to enable them to tackle their own burdens of loneliness, inadequacy, fear and selfishness so that they can begin to face the world-wide horrors that face us all? Jesus can free us from all this. By enabling us to love, to forgive, to accept one another; by showing us a peace of mind that is stronger than that offered by human success; by giving us the assurance that we are, each

'Perhaps it is because we are fearful of one another'

one of us, truly loved by God. And the church, remember, *is* Jesus: 'Saul, Saul, why are you persecuting *me?*'

The Council recognised that if the people of God were to be truly the visible sign of Christ's presence in the world then they must live as *servants of the world*. Aristides recognised this feature of the early Christians ('they never fail to help') and in another of the Vatican Council documents, *The Church in the Modern World*, the bishops spelt out something of what that might mean in the world of to-day:

> Some nations, often with a majority of citizens
> calling themselves Christians,
> enjoy an abundance of the world's goods
> while others are deprived
> of the necessities of life,
> and suffer from hunger, disease,
> and every kind of misery.
> This is a scandal which must end.
> The spirit of poverty and charity
> is the glory and the sign
> of the Church of Christ.

And in other places the Council mentions injustice, racism, disunity in all its forms, as evils which Christians must strive to eradicate as part of their witness to Jesus Christ.

It is this life of Jesus which the church brings to all men and women. She is the visible sign of his presence in the world. She is the living reality of the church founded by Jesus to be his witnesses. She is Catholic, which means that her membership and her mission field is universal, that she is the fulfilment, the embodiment of faith.

In her sacraments the church offers us all a celebration of Christ's presence in us and in our lives. Through them she heals, forgives, strengthens, encourages and rejoices, with the power of Christ. Her role as sacrament, as servant, as pilgrim, as the body of Christ in the world, is to make her Lord visible amidst the pain, anxiety, sufferings, sinfulness, doubts and fears of this world. She cannot do this successfully unless we, her members, recognise her in ourselves. As long as we think of the church as something out there, a building, a pope, a list of rules, a club, she isn't truly being herself. We, through our baptism, are the church. It is in us that Christ must been seen at work, in our gentleness and compassion, our thirst for justice and forgiveness, our integrity and honesty, our love for God, our joy and our faith, that the world will recognise Jesus Christ. Anyone who is worried about the church and her failure to live up to her reality as the body of Christ, the people of God, should ask themselves the question: am *I* part of the problem?

Some young people still feel uncertain about the church. They believe in God, but find much of the church difficult to cope with. She seems unfair in her treatment of women, unclear about war and peace, often politically repressive. So they hesitate to identify themselves wholly with her.

Which brings us back to our first question: what *is* the church? Many children go through a period of disillusionment with their parents. Having looked up to them as knowing everything and always being right, a boy or girl then discovers, sometimes as a shock, that their parents are often wrong, sinful and uncertain. It may take a while for a child to adjust fully to this and to realise that his mother and father are not perfect but they are his parents, and that they belong to each other and that he loves them.

Perhaps something similar happens in our understanding of the church. For Catholics believe that Jesus founded the Church, calling the Apostles to be its first members and teachers. We believe also that what we call the Catholic church to-day is that selfsame church, founded by Jesus, bringing his life to the world. And yet that church is often sinful, foolish and stubborn, hiding rather than revealing Christ. And so we are confused, perhaps disillusioned. But, as Peter said to Jesus, where else can we go? For she is Christ's body, we belong to her, *we are* the church.

It is such a difficult yet important step to see the church as 'we' rather than as 'them'. It is because I, among so many others, am ignorant, selfish, opiniated and mean that the church is too. For I am the church, and I need to recognise that I belong, and make the necessary commitment.

'She seems unfair in her treatment of women'

III. The Pope, Cardinals and Bishops

I'm never quite sure what the Pope is supposed to do. When he comes and talks about Jesus or prayer he can be quite inspiring; but then he goes on and on about contraception and sex and nuns' habits and you wonder what it all means. Do you have to believe everything he says?

The Pope is the bishop of Rome. In the earliest days of the church each local community had its leader, later called a bishop, and it gradually came to be recognised that as the number of local churches grew and multiplied it was necessary to have a centre of unity to which all could belong so as to ensure that each church taught the same doctrine and so was faithful to the witness of the Apostles and the scriptures. Rome was the obvious centre, both because it was almost literally the centre of the known world and the Roman Empire, and also because traditionally St. Peter had been the first bishop of Rome and St. Paul had also taught and died there. So the bishop of Rome became the recognised head of the church.

St. Peter wasn't called the Pope in his life time but the church has held to the tradition that he was the first bishop of Rome. The position of the Pope as we know it today gradually evolved as the church grew bigger and so more complicated. One of the earliest problems was the question of belief and heresy. Who could decide whether Jesus was truly God or, as a strong group of Christians held, only a man doing God's work? So when such crises arose it was the custom to call together as many bishops as possible to discuss and decide on the matter in question. The decision of the bishops (their assemblies came to be called ecumenical councils) was generally ratified by the

32 The Pope, Cardinals and Bishops

bishop of Rome, the Pope. He was looked upon as the sign of unity in the church.

During the Middle Ages the Pope became a ruler of large territories and an important figure in the political movements of Europe especially. He made and unmade kings and emperors and was inclined to claim the right to an interest and a say in the internal affairs of different nations. It wasn't until the later years of the nineteenth century that the Pope finally lost his secular territories and became only a spiritual leader of the church, operating from a tiny piece of ground in Italy, known as the Vatican, and also a sovereign and independent state.

One important question about the Pope is his infallibility. The first thing to be clear about is that it refers primarily to the infallibility of the *church*. This means that the church relies on Jesus' promise both to send her the Holy Spirit 'to lead you into all truth', and that 'the gates of Hell will not prevail against her'. In other words the church believes that the Holy

'He made and unmade kings'

Spirit will not allow her to be led astray in her essential beliefs. The church believed this for centuries, and she also believed that as the Pope was the head of the church, and the sign of unity for the church, he had the right and duty both to ratify the findings of ecumenical councils and to speak in the name of the church if occasion demanded it. All this was explicitly affirmed at the First Vatican Council of 1870, which also laid down that such infallibility was only guaranteed when used explicitly in matters relating to faith and morals.

A Council gets its authority from our belief that Jesus founded a Church. 'You are Peter and on this rock I will build my Church. And the gates of the underworld can never hold out against it. I will give you the keys of the kingdom of heaven: whatever you bind on earth shall be considered bound in heaven; whatever you loose on earth shall be considered loosed in heaven' (Matthew 16.17ff). And, at the end of Matthew's gospel, 'Go, make disciples of all the nations; baptise them in the name of the Father and of the Son and of the Holy Spirit, and teach them to observe all the commands I gave you. And know that I am with you always; yes, to the end of time'.

All of which suggests that the Apostles were given the authority to baptise and to teach, to form a community of followers of Jesus and to teach them how to live; in other words, to found what we would call a church: the people of God (the baptised) living a life of unity with Christ and with each other. Christ's added promise was that he would be with them always, and, as St. John's gospel tells us, that the Holy Spirit would be sent by the Father 'who will lead you to the complete truth'.

Different Christian churches have varying understandings of how the Spirit speaks to the people of God. The Catholic church believes that the Spirit speaks through the baptised but that his guidance is articulated through the bishops, the successors of the Apostles, whether gathered together in council or speaking through their head, the bishop of Rome, whom we call the Pope. In other words, the Pope and the bishops must listen to what the Spirit is saying to the church, and he may at different times speak through individuals (one can think of great saints:

'One can think of great saints: St. Francis for example'

St. Francis, for example), or through movements in the church (the present renewal movement; Cardijn's Young Christian Workers, the base communities of South America; the spirituality of St. Thérèse of Lisieux; the followers of Charles de Foucauld, to name some chosen more or less at random). It is for the Pope and the bishops, what we call the 'magisterium' of the church, to remind us constantly of what the gospel is calling us to, to recognise the authentic voice of the Spirit in such movements, to warn, to advise, to encourage and to teach.

For sometimes such movements are wrong or misguided or untimely. At the beginning of this century, when the church was wrestling with the problems of belief posed by the new theories of Darwin and the new schools of Biblical criticism which replaced the centuries old belief that the Bible was literally true, there arose a movement called Modernism which attempted to relate the faith and teachings of the church with the new understandings. It went too far and so weakened the credibility of the church that it was condemned by Pope Pius X.

The church also understands that she has a mission to guide us in more personal matters. For Jesus told us that if we would love him and share the life of his Father to which we were called it was necessary that we should keep his commandments. The gospels make it plain that the commandments to which he constantly referred were not simply the Ten Commandments of the Old Testament. If you read the sermon on the mount in St. Matthew's gospels you can see this clearly when Jesus expounds on the meaning of those commandments, telling us that not only must we not kill but we must not hate or despise one another, and he repeatedly tells us that we must love one another, 'even as I have loved you'. The beatitudes, again in St. Matthew, provide yet another fresh look at the road on which Jesus is calling us to travel: 'Happy are the meek, the pure of heart, the peacemakers, the poor in spirit...'.

How are we to be sure that we are living our daily lives in harmony with God's will for us? Of course, regular prayer keeps us close to God and less likely to drift away from him, but we still need help and guidance in many personal matters and the church has always understood that the command she received from Christ to teach all nations included the right and duty to offer guidelines on how to interpret the scriptures and how to distinguish between right and wrong in our daily lives. The church offers those guidelines in the teachings and writings of the popes and the Councils and the local bishops and priests. To be able to give such guidance is part of the office to which such men have been called by the church.

This is not the whole story, of course. We each have a conscience and Cardinal Newman tells us that God speaks to us all individually through our consciences which are our precious and sensitive guides to keeping in harmony with God in our lives. But consciences are not magical voices: they are the combination of reason, understanding and faith working together within us and listening to the voice of God. And reason and understanding need to be fed. So we need to read, listen and learn about the things of God: guidance, in other words. So our consciences have to be informed.

As an example, let us look at the vexed question of contraception. The teaching of the church is that artificial methods of birth control are not in harmony with the law of God. A married couple have come to the conclusion that they cannot cope with any more children. What are they to do? They study the teachings of the church and find that although the church does not permit artificial methods of contraception she does accept that the decision to have no more children may well be a moral and good decision and recommends the use of natural methods of birth control. So the couple try such methods and find, perhaps, that for them they do not work. They try abstaining from sex altogether and find the consequences are very bad both for themselves and for their children. They then find that Cardinal Heenan said that Catholics who could not live up to the full requirements of the church over the matter of contraception should not despair but should do their best, and should consider themselves full members of the church and continue to go to the sacraments. They probably discuss all this with their priest and then make a decision together, based on prayer, as to what their consciences tell them to do. If they decide to use a method of contraception not approved by the church such a decision

The Pope, Cardinals and Bishops 37

would need to be constantly reviewed by the couple.

A word about cardinals. They are generally bishops chosen by the Pope to help him in his work. Some are diocesan bishops while others work in the Vatican looking after various aspects of the church's work. They have the responsibility of electing a new Pope when one has died, and have done this since the eleventh century.

Sometimes, with so many important people and so much pomp and ceremony, it may seem that the church is out of touch with the lives of ordinary Catholics and inclined to hide behind positions of authority and bureaucratic structures. Sometimes she is impersonal, harsh and unfair in her actions. Which reminds us that she is human, composed of human beings, not in themselves infallible, and subject to the many limitations we humans possess.

For we must remember that she is only infallible when the whole church is in agreement over a matter of grave importance concerning faith or morals, such agreement being expressed by

'A word about cardinals'

38 The Pope, Cardinals and Bishops

a decision of all the bishops in communion with the Pope, or by the Pope acting as president of the universal college of bishops and in fidelity to the tradition of the church. In other matters, while the church has the duty to teach and to guide and therefore may expect to be listened to and obeyed, she may nevertheless makes mistakes both in the way she does things and in the matter of her rulings.

Let us not forget that the church is a pilgrim church. She is on the way, being led to the fullness of Christ, and she has not got there yet. She is in constant need of reconciliation and renewal, as is every individual Catholic Christian. She needs to learn to be generous, understanding and forgiving in her actions and in her judgements, and to treat all her members, and all men and women, as Christ treated them.

IV. The Mass

I find going to mass on Sundays pretty pointless. It's always the same, it seems dreary and I never get much out of it. I enjoy it far more if I go on a weekday.

When I'm on holiday, if at all possible, I like to slip into some strange (to me) Catholic church on a Sunday morning and attend mass from a bench near the back. It is interesting, and I find it helpful to experience what it must be like from the congregation's point of view. As a priest one is accustomed to having the best seats and the best view.

My impressions are mixed. It often seems very over-verbalised —three readings, a psalm, a sermon, more or less on top of one another, can be quite difficult to follow, let alone reflect on. I like singing at mass and the standard, the quality, the amount, the hymns themselves, vary enormously wherever I happen to be. I sometimes marvel at the faith and perseverance of people

'Let us not forget that the church is a pilgrim church'

who are at mass Sunday after Sunday, often in cramped and uncomfortable pews or benches or chairs, listening to unexceptional sermons, and I wonder if I could have stuck it so loyally if I were not a priest. But it does make me reflect on why people go to mass.

I suppose it was the fear of going to hell if I didn't go to mass that made me attend pretty regularly as a boy. I remember the first time I failed to get to mass on a Sunday. I was about eighteen at the time and on holiday with a friend (not a Catholic). I felt so guilty and scared (and of my mother finding out, too) that I couldn't wait to get to confession the following Saturday. And doubtless there are people who still suffer from the same fear and guilt if they miss mass. So, perhaps as a sort of insurance policy, they make sure that they are always there. My first realisation that there was much wrong with this attitude came in Ireland in the early 1950's.

There was a chapel there which was used by the local parish as an overflow on Sundays. But the local boys used to sit on the steps outside the back of the church and play cards during mass. When remonstrated with by the priest they replied that they had come to church, being obliged to do so, and so what was he worrying about? It must have been soon after that that young people especially stopped going regularly to mass if they didn't want to and ceased to believe that, if they did, they would inevitably end up in hell. I must say, speaking as a priest who has often had to say mass for a reluctant congregation of adolescents, that I was sometimes tempted to suggest that anyone who didn't want to be there had much better leave the church so that the rest of us could get on with it more happily.

People sometimes ask whether it is still a mortal sin not to go to mass on Sundays. The church has done a fair amount of reflective thinking on what constitutes a mortal sin in recent years and is now less inclined to produce lists and categories of sins. She is more inclined to emphasise serious areas of behaviour and attitudes and expect that people will inform their own consciences sincerely and act responsibly, bearing in mind the teaching and the guidelines offered by the church, but making their own decisions.

'...often in cramped and uncomfortable pews
and benches'

But she does still expect Catholics to go to mass on Sundays, not so much as an obligation, rather more as a celebration, a word I had better explain. The church no longer sees herself as an isolated, embattled, élite body, removed from the world and its cares. She now understands that each baptised Christian is part of the people of God, called by God through baptism to be a witness in the world of the love and forgiveness which God has brought to our world through the incarnation, the life and death of Jesus as a man among us. She recognises that through baptism we are made one with Jesus; that he comes with his Father and the Holy Spirit and makes his dwelling place within us; that we are, then, as St. Paul tells us, part of the Body of Christ. And as part of that Body we are truly one, bound together by the life of Christ which lives in you and lives in me. So that we can truly say together 'Our Father', meaning that we are brothers and sisters of Jesus Christ with God as our Father.

One part of our experience cries out against this. We seem to be in opposition to one another rather than truly part of the one Body of Christ. But the church also understands her role today as a pilgrim church, a body of people growing and journeying towards God. So that in one way we are already one with

'Anyone who didn't want to be there had much better leave'

Christ, but in another way, because of our sins and weaknesses, we still have a long way to go on our spiritual journey. And that is really, I suppose, why Christ founded a church at all—because he knew that we would need help, help from God and help from each other, if we were to persevere on our journey. The Old Testament gives a fascinating account of what sort of tangles the Israelites got into in their various wanderings, and we are surely no different and certainly no better.

Hence our church, founded by Christ ('On this rock I will build my Church'), as the community, the people, chosen by God, given faith, and entrusted with the precious burden of carrying the word of God to the rest of the world ('Go and teach all nations'; 'I will be with you till the end of the world'). But he didn't just leave his church to get on with the task by themselves. He gave us the Holy Spirit, and we have the remarkable account in the Acts of the Apostles of the first Pentecost and the way it changed the lives of the first disciples so that they were no longer afraid but had the strength and the conviction to go and face the world with the message of Jesus.

Jesus not only promised us the Holy Spirit, but he also left us a visible sign of his constant presence in our hearts. You must be familiar with the various accounts of the Last Supper, when Jesus took bread and wine, broke the bread, blessed it, and gave it to his disciples, telling them that it was his body and his blood. And he had already told them, as reported in St. John's gospel, that unless they ate his body and drank his blood they could not share his eternal life. And he added the command: 'Do this, in memory of me'.

It is important to be clear about what Jesus was doing. In the first place he was making an offering of himself to God the Father. You will remember that to offer sacrifice means to make something holy and therefore acceptable. Well, Jesus was offering himself, and the point of his offering was that he was truly God and so his offering was perfect, holy, and complete; and he was also truly man so that we, being men and women too, *shared* in his offering. In other words, he was able to make us holy and acceptable to God so long as we remain in union with him. That offering of Jesus we call Christ's sacrifice on the cross, his identification with us; and hence the pain, the suffering, and the death—because we were all marred with sin and it took the totality of Christ's love to overcome our sin and selfishness, greed and pride, lust and envy and meanness of spirit. He put himself, quite literally, into our hands and our sinfulness rejected him. But he didn't abandon us. He offered himself for us, he was one of us, and God was able to accept him and his offering *on our behalf*. So it was a perfect offering, acceptable to God, because it was the offering of Jesus Christ. And it made all men and women holy and acceptable to God. Heaven is open to us, is our destiny, our hope and our joy, because we are one with Jesus *and for no other reason*. Without Jesus we are still stuck in our sins.

It is important to remember that Jesus was truly a human being, a man. He understands us men and women, not only because he created us but also because he has shared our lives. And he realised that we would need constant help if we were to be faithful to the mission he gave us. So not only did he send the Holy Spirit on to all the baptised, but he also gave us this special gift of himself, in the bread and the wine, in what we call a sacrament (an outward, visible sign of the inner, invisible spiritual reality), so that we could have the constant, regular reminder of his presence, and of our unity with him and with each other, whenever we shared the bread and the cup, his body and blood.

One thing the Catholic church has always been absolutely constant in is her belief in the real presence of Jesus in the eucharist. Many other Christian bodies have tried to water it down, talking only of signs and symbols and representations and spiritual realities and the like, but I suppose what it boils down to is that the church has tried to remain absolutely faithful to the tradition she received from the Apostles, and which she has always believed, namely, that Jesus identified himself with the bread and the wine when he said, 'Take, and eat, this is my body, given for you'. This may seem difficult but, after all, if God could identify himself with the blood, bones and flesh of a human being, presumably it is no more difficult for him to identify himself with bread and wine.

There's a remarkable account in the sixth chapter of St. John's gospel of how Jesus tried to prepare the Jews for the eucharist. He hammers home the point that he will give his body and blood for the life of the world and that they must eat and drink it if they wish to share his life. And not surprisingly many of them turned away in disgust and walked with him no more. He seemed to be preaching cannibalism and they simply couldn't take it. But the Apostles stayed. I'm sure they didn't understand either but they did trust Jesus so they stayed with him. As Peter said: 'Where else should we go? You have the words of eternal life'. And that is the position held by the Catholic church. Of course we do not *understand* but we do *believe*. We believe the words of Jesus, and we believe in the testimony of the church which has remained faithful to this belief, handed down by Matthew, Mark and Luke, expounded by Paul, treasured by men and women in the church for nearly two thousand years. In the eucharist Jesus gives us himself, not a sign merely, nor a reminder, but himself, so that we can say with confidence that he is truly present in the eucharistic gifts, and so we treat them with reverence and awe. To believe doesn't mean that we have to understand, but rather that we are asked to trust and to love. On the road to Emmaus the disciples recognised Jesus when he broke bread with them; we are asked by him to do the same: to recognise him when we share the bread and the wine of the eucharist, for he is truly there.

So we come together on Sundays; the day, incidentally, on which the first Christians used to meet to rejoice because it was the day of Jesus' resurrection from the dead, and so a special day for them. We come together on Sundays to do two things: first of all to share in the eucharistic meal, the meal that makes us truly one with God and one with each other (hence the name: communion), and in which our offering is acceptable to God, the offering of all that we have to bring to mass. It may not seem much: a week's work, play, generosity, but marred by selfishness, apathy and sin; but because we are one with Jesus our pitiful little offering becomes one with his offering and so is acceptable to God.

And, secondly, we come together as a church, as a visible

body of believing Christians, proclaiming before the world, and in union with each other, what we believe and hold most precious. So we come to help one another, to say the creed together, to pray together, to greet one another, to make our offering together, above all to receive communion together, as an affirmation that we are one in the spirit, that we belong to each other. The mass is not a private devotion, a silent coming together to pray, it is a *celebration*, with Christ in the midst of us; it is a *thanksgiving* ('eucharist' is a Greek word meaning just that) for what God has done for us; it is a *communion*, in which we share a common meal which binds us together, as indeed do all shared meals (birthdays, anniversaries, friends to supper, breaking bread together); and it is a *sacrifice*, in which we share in Christ's offering of himself, an offering so perfect that it makes the world holy because he is one with us, one of us.

And it has a third purpose, too. 'Mass' means to be *sent*, and just as Jesus washed the feet of his first disciples at the Last Supper and told them to go and do likewise, so we are sent away from each mass to bring God's healing love and service to our world. The eucharist is something that we *do* and *live* rather than something that we just attend and yawn at—no wonder we find it boring! It involves a commitment.

Young people often find mass boring but I expect you, and many others, have attended *some* masses, perhaps at retreats, youth days, papal visits or house masses, when something of that spirit has been present and been recognised.

When the first Christians met in each other's houses on Sunday evenings to celebrate mass they used to strengthen each other's faith by reading passages from the scriptures, from the letters of Paul, and with the president preaching to them. It was obviously much more informal than nowadays, but as the church grew and spread it became more necessary to develop a fixed form for the mass so that it would be fully part of the church's traditional beliefs. And, as you have doubtless discovered, whereas a certain informality is helpful and easy to achieve in a small group having mass in someone's room, it is a very different matter with large numbers of people in large churches. Then a greater solemnity and dignity is helpful, microphones are probably necessary, time limits have to be kept to (with another mass likely to be following at a fixed time), and so forth.

And so the more or less fixed formula of the mass emerged, made universally uniform at the Council of Trent in the sixteenth century, translated into different languages, and made a little more flexible once more at the Second Vatican Council.

But the important point that has to be made here is that our celebration of the mass is more or less bound to be what we decide to make of it. I know that many young people enjoy folk liturgies, with lots of good hymns and an informal atmosphere that is none the less prayerful and reverent for being informal. But surely it is true that one reason for the greater sense of enjoyment in such a mass is that everyone is fully participating, singing wholeheartedly, listening with attention, concentrating in the still, silent moments, trying to make a real offering of themselves with Jesus: in other words, when everyone present has brought a generous commitment to the mass.

'...singing wholeheartedly, listening with attention'

It is not always easy for the priest, either. Do you ever think what it must be like for him, faced with an obviously apathetic congregation, some of whom will sing and some of whom will not; some of whom welcome the sign of peace and some of whom refuse to give it; some there because they want to be, but others clearly completing a not particularly welcome obligation?

Of course, much is often done to help with this problem. In many parishes to-day there are lively liturgical groups that help the priests to prepare and celebrate the liturgy of the parish, often bearing in mind the varied needs of the different age-groups, but working hard to make the liturgy the central celebration that binds the parish together as a real sector of the people of God.

We still have to face the fact that all is not well liturgically, or perhaps in a number of other ways, with our parishes generally, or with many priests too. The renewal of the church since the Second Vatican Council has been patchy and partial, although I am encouraged to be told that it took the church a hundred years to accept the Council of Trent, which took place during the Reformation in the sixteenth century. Many priests neither understand nor sympathise with the renewed rites of mass and the sacraments, and they have little patience with young people who are eager for more meaningful celebrations.

But do not be depressed by this. First of all, be sure that you yourself understand what you are doing at mass. Secondly, find a friend and talk it over together. Thirdly, go and have a chat with your parish priest, not in a critical or threatening way, but simply showing an interest and a readiness to help and to get involved.

It may not work. It may be that you and a small number of friends may have to soldier on without much help or encouragement. But you can help each other, especially by praying together, by joining in young people's events in the diocese, by realising clearly that you are bringing your life to God with Jesus at mass and that he is accepting your offering and making it and you holy. This is being a mature Catholic which God is clearly asking you to be.

'...some of whom welcome the sign of peace and some of whom refuse to give it'

V. Confession

It's ages since I've been to confession. I wouldn't know what to say. And, anyway, surely God forgives my sins if I tell him I'm sorry?

Of course he does. But I suppose one of your problems is that you were taught how to go to confession at about the age of seven, before making your first communion, and that you very soon established a regular list of sins that didn't vary much whenever you went to confession: 'told lies, forgot my morning and night prayers, swore, was rude, was disobedient', and that it didn't seem to make much difference.

In the Old Testament the word most commonly used to describe sin really means 'to miss the mark', or 'failing to make the mark'. The idea behind this is that we have a goal in life, for Christians our endeavour to 'love the Lord your God with your whole heart, and your whole mind, and your whole strength, and to love your neighbour as yourself'. If we look at our own lives, hopes, achievements in the light of this goal or mark it isn't difficult to see that we are a long way short of it, all the time. That great gap in our lives, between our selfishness and the love which we long for, can be called our sinfulness. It needs forgiveness, healing, making up for, if we are ever to come close to God. From this point of view it is probably more sensible to think about what we haven't done, rather than try to list all our actual sins. In other words, how much actual loving have I done, except when it was convenient for me to do so? How many people who needed something from me, perhaps a smile, or a helping hand, or a bit of my time, received nothing at all or weren't even noticed because I was concentrating all the time on my own comfort? And in the graphic account of the last judgement which Jesus gives in St. Matthew's gospel he makes our response to our neighbour's needs *the* test of our credibility as Christians: 'inasmuch as you did it to the least of these my little ones you did it unto me'.

One difficulty is that you were taught how to go to confession at the age of seven in a way that may have made good sense at that age but which is probably not much help for someone of your age now. Confession is a sacrament, and that means a real, visible moment in our lives when we are touched by the healing love of God, a moment made real and visible by the use of words, actions and signs. Because it is to do with reality it must have a meaningful connection with you and your present state of life. In other words, I would not expect to hear the same sort of confession from an eight year old boy, a twenty year old girl, and a sixty year old man. Yet I often do!

So the first thing to think about when considering confession is what is important to you. What is important to you at this moment? Perhaps it is your looming exams, your friendships, your relations with your family, your boy or girl friend, your sense of failure; what do you value most at this time? What are your ambitions? Where does God come in? What worries you most? Do you feel guilty about anything that you'd like to clear up? What sort of 'mark' are you aiming for? What sort of a Christian do you want to be?

If you haven't been to confession for a long time and would like to start again I suggest you ask a priest if you might have a chat with him, perhaps leading to confession. You may well have a friend who has done this and can recommend a priest who is used to this sort of confession. Then, be quite open with the priest. Tell him that it is years since your last confession, that you don't know what to say or where to begin, and that you're very nervous indeed. He will help you begin to talk about yourself.

Some people are worried that if they are honest in confession the priest will despise them, but suppose a friend came to you and begged your help in a shameful situation where she was guilty. Would you condemn and despise her? Or would you not rather admire her courage and frankness and be anxious to help her all you could? And the priest has a further advantage because he knows from experience that all we human beings are very much the same and all have the same guilty and furtive areas of our lives, particularly in anything to do with sex, the only difference being that some are honest enough to admit it and others are not. My own experience is to be full of genuine admiration for anyone who can make an honest and frank confession.

Someone once gave another description of sin: 'of being in the wrong relationship—with other people or with God'. I suppose that's true of a lot of us much of the time. Sometimes the solution is obvious: to go and say that we are sorry and make it up with the person concerned. That often brings healing and joy. But generally it isn't as simple as that. For a start, we *belong* to the church. That means that we are in a relationship with very many people. Indeed, as we call God our Father, we can say, can we not, that we are brothers and sisters to everyone else whom God has made. A lot of the time, sometimes without caring about it at all, we neglect, ignore, hurt other people. Often we don't even know that we have done so. Yet we have done so and we do need to be reconciled. That is one reason why we start mass with a rite of reconciliation, for Jesus tells us: 'if you have anything against your brother, leave your gift at the altar, and go and be reconciled with your brother'. In the early years of Christianity people used to come and be reconciled publicly in church. Yet there is still a need to be reconciled to God and to his church, our fellow pilgrims and children of God.

There are further implications in belonging to the church. We live in a world in which injustice seems to abound. Many people squander rich resources in greed and waste while others simply starve. We know that a fraction of what the western world spends on defence could save the lives of millions who will die of starvation. We realise that the very structures of our industrial, consumer society are inclined to make the rich richer and the poor poorer. In the face of this we feel helpless, and yet to some extent we are involved. We are part of what is called the 'social' sin of mankind and our silence and acquiescence do involve us in the guilt. For that too we need to ask God's forgiveness.

It is important to understand that God isn't too worried about your daily list of faults. As I said earlier, he has made you so that you can learn to love him and become one with him. And our road to that love lies in learning how to love each other. Jesus is asking a lot of each one of us: really listening to one another, supporting, helping and working for. And not only my friends. The gospel story of the good Samaritan is worth really pondering over. Who *is* my neighbour?

When I think of all the people I have hurt or neglected or deliberately ignored; when I see the injustices in the world in which I live, I begin to recognise my need for forgiveness from God, and for reconciliation with both God and my fellow men. How is this to be done?

Since its earliest times the church found it necessary to have a leader in each small church community and these leaders very soon came to be called bishops. So in order to be reconciled with all one's fellow Christians it became necessary to be reconciled with one's own bishop—he was the acknowledged leader, teacher, pastor and spokesman for the local church: and he still is. If reconciled to him through the visible sacramental rite of confession, the Christian was truly reconciled through the grace of God, with all his fellows. The priest helps the bishop in his work in the Christian local communities. If you want to find the Catholic church in any part of the world you will probably start by finding the priest. So he represents the whole Body of Christ when he receives you in the sacrament of confession, which we now, more meaningfully, call reconciliation.

I've talked about failing to make the mark, about the need for reconciliation. There is also the need for specific forgiveness, perhaps one of the deepest needs we all have. Often we forgive and are forgiven by our friends and we know how important it is if our friendship is going to thrive. Above all we need God's forgiveness for our sins. We can be confident that we are forgiven by God if we are sorry in our hearts. But God founded a visible church, a visible community of baptised Christians, bound in a visible unity by the sharing of the consecrated bread and wine, the Body and Blood of Christ.

He could have made an invisible church, simply telling us to love God and go our separate ways. But he told his followers to go and baptise, to bless and break the bread, to teach all nations. He knew that we, being human, needed visible dimensions to our life as Christians. And in the sacramental absolution we have a visible, dimensional act of being touched by the forgiving grace of God. We know that we are forgiven and such visible, sacramental experience helps us on our road to God. Does not an involved, shared, meaningful eucharist help us as weak human beings? Very few people can get safely to God without such visible aids. And Jesus did tell us to use them. So as the eucharist celebrates God's sacrifice on our behalf, the sacrament of reconciliation *celebrates* our forgiveness by God.

There is a further dimension to the sacrament. If we are serious about trying to be Christians, trying how to learn to love God and each other, in a world that seems to be increasingly secular and selfish in its preoccupations, we probably need guidance, encouragement and advice. Some sort of spiritual direction. If you use confession in the way I have suggested, by going to a priest and having a chat, you will find that he can help you to discover what are your values, in what sort of direction you are heading. He can help you to pray; he can advise you about worrying matters of conscience; he can be a real sort of soul friend, someone you can trust and with whom you can be completely open and honest. There is a freedom and a joy in being able to talk about oneself in such a way to someone whom one can trust and who understands—and that is an essential part of his ministry as a priest: to *minister to*, to help all Christians on their journey to God.

So, how often? Obviously not every week. That sort of serious discussion can only be held at fairly lengthy intervals. I should suggest at least three lengthy confessions each year—perhaps before Christmas, before Easter and after the long summer holidays: perhaps at the start of the autumn session if you are a student. That is only a suggestion. Some can only manage once a year, perhaps when on a short retreat. In addition I think it helps to make shorter, simpler confessions whenever you feel

'If you use confession in the way I have suggested by going to a priest and having a chat'

the need. I might add that if you can find a priest to whom you can go regularly, so that he gets to know you well, there are obvious advantages.

If you are anxious or shy or embarrassed about talking to a priest it might help to go into a confessional box in a church in the usual way and ask the priest if it would be possible to come and talk to him sometime. If he can't do it he will never know who you are and you can try another priest. And don't let us forget that some people still prefer the anonymity of the confessional box and, especially for those who are fearful or embarrassed or who haven't taken to confession for a long time, it is often the best method and it is still and should always be widely available.

'Some people still prefer the anonymity of the confessional box'

VI. Confirmation

Confirmation to me meant a very long tedious ceremony by the bishop. At eleven years of age could it really have been expected to mean much more?

Yes, I was confirmed at the age of eight and remember even less of the occasion. What you say about it generally being given too young would be echoed by many today.

In the early days of the church, as far as we can ascertain the matter, confirmation seems to have been given at the same time as baptism. As most baptisms were conferred on adults this must have seemed the obvious way to do it. The same thing happens today when an adult is received into the church. He is confirmed by the priest who receives him. So I suppose the first question we need to think about is why have infant baptism?

For many centuries the baptised child had the promises made in its name by the parents and godparents, and it was then generally considered that at confirmation the child more or less accepted the baptismal promises made on its behalf. So confirmation came not long after first confession and communion which were given at the age of reason, at about seven years old. It was also generally believed that an unbaptised baby, if it died, would be incapable of entering heaven as it had been baptised neither by water, nor by desire (for it was too young to have been capable of any form of rational acts of will), nor by blood, the blood of martyrdom. So what would happen to it? No one really knew, and moral theologians thought up the idea of limbo, a place of rest for unbaptised souls, and obviously greatly inferior to heaven as there was no place in limbo for enjoying the vision of God. Not unnaturally parents were most anxious to preserve their babies from the possibility of such a fate and so had them baptised at the earliest possible opportunity. Since then the church has thought again about the theology of limbo and the general belief today is that its existence is, to say the least, doubtful, Most theologians would agree that the fate of the unbaptised baby can be safely left in God's hands, so there is less pressure for an immediate baptism of an infant.

But it is still the practice to baptise babies, and for a very good reason. The church is increasingly understood as the people of God, a body to which we all belong by reason of our baptism, and a body the members of which are united in their common faith and love for God, and bound together in a special way by their sharing in the body of Christ in the eucharist. Would you leave the children out of this? I often wonder what the parents did when Jesus was among them? Did they leave them at home (to decide about it when they grew up), or did they bring them along from the start and make sure they shared in anything that Jesus was doing? And he himself said 'suffer the little children to come unto me'. So it is customary, and surely desirable, to baptise the babies into the family of the church.

But there has been a distinct change in the wording of the sacrament. The promises are now made by the parents and godparents, not in the name of the child, but as promises in their own names; affirmations of their own faith, a renewal of their own baptismal promises, and a commitment to try to bring the child up in the knowledge and practice of the Christian faith.

Which leaves confirmation as the subject of a fair amount of debate. We understand the sacrament to mean the very special gift of the Holy Spirit, through the laying on of hands, the most ancient of Christian ceremonies for the invoking of the Holy Spirit; and the anointing with the oil of chrism, the oil of dedication and commitment, the oil used for the anointing of priests and bishops when they are ordained to share in Christ's priestly work.

Although lay people are not ordained priests they get the same anointing because the church has taken very seriously St. Peter's description of the baptised Christian as part of a 'royal priesthood', 'a people set apart', to offer spiritual sacrifices acceptable to God'. All this means that through baptism

'But it is still the practice to baptise babies'

we share in the life, death and resurrection of Jesus; we become truly one with him. So we are called to share in his priesthood. And the priestly job is to offer sacrifice, a word which, quite simply, means to make holy. Jesus came to make the world holy, because it was only if it were made holy that it could become acceptable to God. He gave his life for that purpose.

We, then, as baptised Christians, sharing in Christ's priestly life, are called on to make the world holy. And we do that by living our lives in as close a harmony as we can with the will of God, by living generously, truthfully, at one with God. When we are doing that we can make everything we do holy, whether it is working for an exam, typing in an office, cooking the lunch, playing football, walking with our friends, or whatever it may be. Because we are one with Christ through our baptism we possess his power within us, his power to change the indifferent into the holy.

'...whether it is working for an exam, typing in an office, cooking the lunch'

Baptism is the sacrament of initiation into that life, but because, for the reasons outlined above, it is generally considered better to baptise in infancy, the obvious moment of anointing, or commitment, to that life as a member of the royal priesthood of Christ, is when we are confirmed by the bishop of our diocese, set apart to share in Jesus' mission of making the world holy and acceptable to God. Which is, of course, a solemn moment in our lives and one which should, I suppose, be entered upon freely and with a real sense of making a commitment of ourselves to God.

What would be the best age for that? One reason for choosing eleven was that it was, for most children, the end of primary education and often the end of Catholic schooling. So all children could be properly prepared for what we call the sacraments of initiation while still at Catholic schools, with the hope that it would also help them to face the more demanding challenges of secondary education and adolescence. But many young people really reach the difficult time at about fourteen or fifteen. That is when they need help and in some dioceses that is now when they are being confirmed. With the help of schools, parishes and parents a real effort is being made to make this a meaningful moment of choice and dedication in the life of the young Catholic, a time when her real adult life as a Catholic begins.

But there are still problems. Many young people stop going to church after this age and some only start getting interested in religion again in the upper sixth form or even later. So is there any ideal age for confirmation? I suppose you could say that it should be different for every child, and that confirmation should take place when a child asks for it and is ready for it. But if my fourteen year old friends are all being confirmed of course I shall want to be confirmed too. Others would suggest that there should be a fixed age at which all young Catholics would, as it were, be initiated into adulthood as Christians, and that the best time for this would be at fourteen, *before* the most difficult period of adolescence. The Bar Mitzvah for young Jewish boys is generally held at about the age of twelve. Thereafter they are ranked with the men.

I know one girl who told me that she had been confirmed at eleven, lost interest in the church at fifteen but found it again at nineteen, when she would simply love to have been confirmed anew, when it really would have been an adult commitment for her.

But in a way, because we are sinners, we are always longing for a chance to make a fresh start, wishing we could wipe out everything that has happened so far, and re-dedicate ourselves to God with clear consciences. And of course we can. If you remember what I said about the sacrament of reconciliation perhaps you can understand that this is, *par excellence*, the sacrament of renewal, of re-commitment, of making a fresh start? It is a sacrament in which all our sins are forgiven, when all that is lacking in our lives is made up by Jesus, when all our wounds are healed. It asks for an act of sorrow for what has gone before, and an act of dedication to try to live a renewed life from now onwards. The priest, sometimes laying his hands on your head, prays that the Holy Spirit will bring reconciliation and forgiveness. You go forth with all the gifts of the Holy Spirit you received at confirmation renewed. And God, knowing our weakness, has made this sacrament available whenever we need it. And you can make it, in your life, as solemn and important as your confirmation.

There is also the opportunity to renew our baptismal vows publically at the Easter Vigil service on Holy Saturday night. This, again, could be made more of, either individually, or as a family, or a group of friends, or as a parish.

VII. Sex

Father, I have a problem. I went to a party, met a young man, and we grew fond of each other and started to kiss and hug. After a while he started to fondle my breast and I found the warm, tender sensation lovely. Was it wrong?

It wouldn't be difficult to continue the story, or many stories like it. Who to consult? Parents? No, they might be shocked and probably wouldn't understand. The priest in confession? Well, no, I haven't been to confession for ages and what would he think of me? Perhaps a friend. She sympathises, agrees that it is probably all right—after all, the church only specifically forbids sexual intercourse before marriage. But the doubt, although tucked away by now, might remain.

Still, when this has happened a few times, it really does not seem too bad, and so when the next boy (or the same one) goes a bit further and slips his hand between her legs it doesn't seem too dreadful: and he did it because she did not resist too much. So why not spend the night together in bed—though without, of course, having sexual intercourse? It is a lovely experience, tender, loving, sharing. It brings us closer together, deepens our love and respect for each other, we say a prayer together. Guilty feelings? Not really, although it would be nice to know for sure whether it is right or wrong in the eyes of the church. It *seems* all right. And yet, well, the boy was urgent last night and we did masturbate each other. Not quite so sure about that—but, again, it wasn't actual intercourse, and everyone now knows that masturbation isn't really wrong.

And the boy? Well, he loves her, doesn't he? And when she lets him undress her and caress her body it is so lovely that it *can't* be really wrong—and he wouldn't dream of suggesting

'We grew fond of each other and started to kiss and hug'

actual intercourse. Confession? Well, the priest may be old fashioned and not understand, so better not to mention it. Anyway, it's *not* wrong; it's a lovely experience. He wouldn't dream of hurting a hair on her head. Is that a fanciful scenario?

No, Father, it's not. So what are you going to say? I'd love to know how far you can go?

Let's begin with a question? What do you want? What sort of relationships are you looking for in life? Do you want lots of fairly shallow friendships which don't commit you to very much? Or are you hoping one day to find a deep, fulfilling, satisfying love to which you can give your whole self? I'll assume the second is what you want. If that is so, then it presumes that you value truth in your relationships. When someone says to you 'I love you', you are entitled to believe that they are speaking the truth. Admittedly, that alone raises lots of problems. Does he mean he wants to marry you, to be your friend for a while, to persuade you to go to bed with him? Perhaps he doesn't really know himself. But a least let us agree that in matters as important as this we are entitled to expect the truth—that our partners will be trustworthy. Would you agree with that?

Yes, I would, very much so. But it's difficult.

Let me press you further on this. To be true to oneself, to be honest with oneself, with one's family, one's friends, with God—how important is that?

I haven't really thought about it. But it sounds O.K.

Think for a little about truth and wholeness. Being one person and not always having to hide or pretend or worry about being found out. To be able to be oneself, with a clear conscience, to trust and to be trusted, to love and to be loved: perhaps that is what I mean by wholeness. In English the words for whole and holy are very nearly the same. They mean being trustworthy,

66 Sex

meaning what you say, not letting people down, being honest, not devious, open and frank, not furtive and guilty. So let's use this as a background to thinking about sex. Do you want to be honest and trustworthy? To be a whole person?

Of course I do. Which is exactly why I started this conversation.

Well, splendid! For we use our bodies constantly to *communicate*. We smile, frown, grimace, wink, nod and grin; we look up and we turn our backs; we shake hands, touch, kiss and hug: all are important parts of the way we communicate with each other. Years ago, before the so-called permissive society, there was a sort of code of bodily language between girls and boys. In Victorian days it was very strict indeed and a proper kiss meant a proposal of marriage. Thirty years ago it was less rigid but still in use (although not, of course, always kept). Then, holding hands came first; followed by, but not on the first outing, a goodnight kiss; then a more serious kiss; and then arms around each other and a good hugging session. None of this happened at once and there was a general recognition that each step

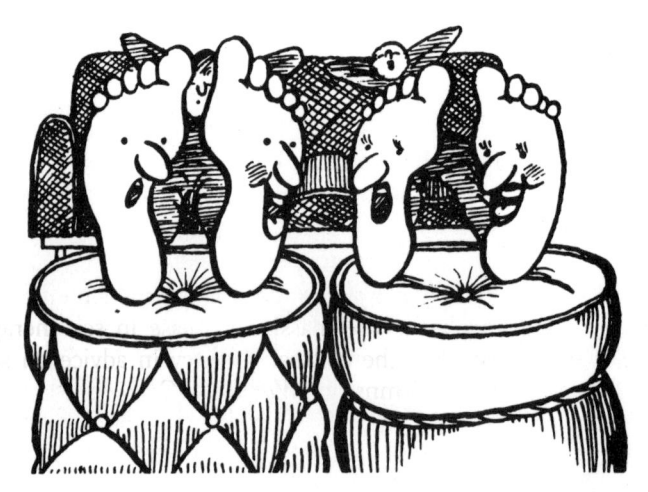

'...for we use our bodies constantly to communicate'

reflected a developing relationship that was special. Does this sound archaic? But although often abused, it was true.

Today the signals seem to be less clear. My observation of sixth form dances, for example, suggests that fondling bodies, breasts included, often comes at the first meeting and is often the substitute for conversation: not a sign of a growing friendship but serving either to satisfy a simple lust or to cover up a mutual embarrassment as neither boy nor girl has anything to say to each other. But beginning with mothers and babies we do recognise that bodily language is enormously important in communicating love, security and support, and most people recognise the difference between the dutiful kiss which is expected on first acquaintance and a warm hug between two friends who are glad to be with each other again. Do you know whom I mean by Hugh Hafner?

The man who founded 'Playboy'? Yes, but what's he got to do with it?

When *Playboy* first appeared, and it was I suppose the pioneer sex magazine, it used to run a forum of letters and articles to discuss what it called the *Playboy* philosophy. This, which seemed a novel idea at the time, was that sex and love do not have much to do with each other. Sex is fun, a pleasurable experience open to all, and requiring no commitment or responsibility providing that both partners are willing. This is now the agreed philosophy of most magazines and sex manuals and indeed of much of the media and perhaps a large proportion of people who live in the western world. Moreover, the modern manuals go further and suggest that if we don't all have lots of sex and especially lots of orgasms then we are sick and in need of treatment, and hence the massive increase in sex therapy clinics in America and the collosal industry in advice on sex ranging from the columns in *Woman's Own* to the ever growing number of sex shops throughout Britain. Do I exaggerate? I think even a cursory examination of any of the magazines widely read by teenagers and young people will confirm this.

So it is against this background that the young Catholic has to struggle to cope with the church's 'no' to sex before marriage.

But surely times have changed. We do know more about sex than the Victorians did.

We certainly talk about it more. But the church is concerned with integrity and truth and being whole and trustworthy, and she believes that bodily language is a means of communication —a delightful, meaningful way of expressing our love for one another. In other words, just as we expect verbal language to be true ('I love you, Mary') so should our bodily language. The evangelists were doubly shocked by Judas' betrayal of Jesus with a 'tender, loving kiss', yet nowadays is a girl sure when a boy kisses her, or even asks her to sleep with him, that the physical experience is a sign of love and affection rather than a shared pleasure using each other's body?

But does this matter? Surely there is a place for both. We can use sex for fun and also for serious, committed relationships.

But can we? One of the results of the *Playboy* philosophy has been to drive a wedge between the sexual side of men and women and the loving, committed, relationship side. So that it is considered normal for a man to look for sexual satisfaction with any girl, or even with the aid of pictures, books or films. Normal, that is, not for a teenager struggling to cope with his own growing sexual awareness, but for a so-called mature adult. Yet surely the normal, mature adult should be a person whose sexual desires are in harmony with his love and commitment of which they are an expression? Yet a man or woman today who maintains that fidelity in relationships is precious and the only way to complete human integrity (when what I say with my body is in complete harmony with what I say with my mind and heart) is considered old fashioned and possibly even prudish or frigid. Of course sex should be fun, but only where it is completely honest.

But lots of my friends sleep with one another and are still capable of loyal, loving relationships.

Is that the general experience of our time, do you think? Since the acceptance of permissive sex (when you like, with whom you like, providing you both agree) are relationships more stable, people generally happier, children more secure? It could be argued that the last twenty years have seen a big increase in broken marriages (a third now end in divorce), abortions (75,000 in 1970; 128,000 in 1981), unwanted pregnancies and people on vallium. And these aren't just statistics, for they represent men and women struggling to find joy and fulfilment in their lives and their relationships.

Obviously there are complex reasons for these symptoms but who can doubt that the confusion over the meaning of bodily language has not helped. Are girls happy today with this new sexual freedom? Are they content to go on the pill at 16, 'just in case'? Are they confident and secure about their physical relations with boys? I don't think many of them are. There is a lot of guilt, worry, confusion, fear and general uncertainty. A girl may not want sex before marriage but may be very worried that if she constantly says no she will end up with no boyfriends at all.

Are boys that certain about their desire to sleep with the girls they take out? Apart from the urge of the flesh surely many are not. But their fellows and the standards of our age almost force them to take part. It is not easy to stand aloof from the party when everyone is paired with someone else and clothes are coming off all round.

And who is there to talk it over with? Generally, no one at all. So it gets accepted, albeit uneasily; the guilt, if there is any, is suppressed, and they live with a vague hope that God understands even if the church does not. Do boys and girls seriously discuss these question together?

Not very often. Just sometimes, with a close friend.

Not long ago, at a school I know, a co-educational school, a sixth form R.E. class was divided into separate groups of boys and girls and each group was asked to discuss together and write down what they expected from their future partners in marriage. When the two lists were compared they found, to their consternation, that they hardly agreed at all. The girls were looking for love, companionship, tenderness; and the boys wanted someone who would be a good housekeeper, a good mother and good in bed. There seems to be a need for young people really to discover what the other sex is like and to share serious discussions about these vital questions.

O.K. Can we get back to these physical relationships? What is their real importance?

Relationships are about becoming oneself. A child needs to be loved, to be wanted, to belong, in order that he or she can grow securely, happily and fully. And so do we all. We need to be affirmed by others—to be welcomed, to be loved, to know that we matter just for our own sake. When we *know* that we are loved we feel secure and happy, we don't have to pretend any more and so we can become truly ourselves. Without love we tend to be lonely, unsure, frightened of revealing too much, and so remain less than truly ourselves. Does that make sense?

Yes, very much so.

Well, if relationships are about helping one another to become truly ourselves, then they must be genuine, truthful and reliable. How are they expressed? How do they grow? We normally think of relationships growing through verbal means, by what we say to each other. But that is only a small part of it. True, we use words of greeting, words of encouragement, words of support, words of explanation, and so on; but we also use smiles, hugs, kisses, fondling, stroking, where these are appropriate. Should not all these signs and sharing be true? We can see what is wrong in lying to one another verbally. Is it not equally wrong to lie to one another physically? Which is what happens, is it not, if my heart says that I'm quite fond of you

'The boys wanted someone who would be a good housekeeper'

but not yet ready to make a commitment, while my body gives you everything it has and expects the same from you in return?

But does this matter if both partners understand that their physical sharing is not meant to express total commitment?

One of the problems with sexual signs is that the physical expression itself can be so pleasurable and exciting that we are easily drawn to use it for its own sake, for mutual pleasure, and not to express and encourage love: the *Playboy* philosophy. Does this matter?

One day a young man came to see me during his first year at university. He told me that he had found a lovely girl friend, that they were living together, sleeping together, and were entirely happy and guiltless. He said he felt strengthened by the relationship and he was sure it was good. Two years later he came to see me again and said he wanted to tell me the sequel as he had trusted me with the beginning. After a year together he and his girl friend had decided, quite amicably, that the time had come to part. There were no hard feelings and both felt that it had all been very worthwhile. But he soon found that, having become used to a sexual partner in his bed, it wasn't easy to sleep alone again. So he started to look for a girl, any girl, who would move in with him. This time there was no question of love, merely the satisfying of his physical needs. He told me about it because he recognised that as a person he had deteriorated, that fidelity in love was no longer as important to him as sexual satisfaction. I tell this story because it illustrates how easy it is to separate sex from commitment and love and how hard it is to bring the two together again. It also brings us back to the question I asked at the beginning. What do you want?

For if to love and be loved is important then I suggest that the validity of language *is* important. If marriage is a commitment for life, then 'I love you', 'I want you', 'I give myself to you', are crucial statements, and not easy to make from the fullness of our hearts. And the most crucial statement of all is sexual intercourse. It means: 'I am giving you all that I have to give as a sign that we belong to each other and I am wholly committed to you', and this particularly on the first occasion of sexual intercourse, the act that for centuries was understood as the act that made a marriage valid and real.

If it *doesn't* mean that, then what does it mean? And how am I to know? If I am content to use my body simply for pleasure what have I to say or give to the boy or girl whom I do want to marry? Does this sound pedantic or meaningless to you?

No, I don't think so. But go on.

Jesus said: 'happy are the pure in heart'. I suppose to be pure in heart means to be at one with yourself, to be single-minded in your search for truth, and I suppose that, as Christians, we surely do want to be truthful, whole, meaningful in our relationships with one another. And if our words ought to be truthful, so ought our actions. And if this is so then sexual intercourse cannot be separated from the complete commitment of I to You, that which we call marriage, if it is to be wholly true.

But that is hard to live up to. Supposing you get it nearly right, when two people love each other a lot but aren't yet in a position to get married?

Of course our language can be *nearly* true and there is a big difference between sleeping with a casual contact with no commitment at all, which really does seem to be an abasement of the language of love, and sleeping with someone whom we hope or intend to marry. But even the latter case is not wholly true, is it? Something is being held back in the relationship, the commitment is not quite complete—otherwise why not stand up in front of the world and get married? A sexual relationship that belongs to complete commitment is being misused and is not wholly true, if it is used in such a case. So there will be some doubt, some reservation, a nagging worry, a hesitation to speak proudly of it before parents, before the church, and even one's own conscience. The real joy of sex and love and commitment being truly one and completely honest is that it is, quite simply, wholesome, right with the partners, with their families, and with God.

Can I go back to the question I started with? What about the preliminaries in relationships? What is a true use of physical language between a boy and a girl who love each other?

It is not easy to lay down exact, uniform criteria which are equally valid for everyone. The church has always tended to take the safe way and forbid any physical contact that has any real danger of arousing powerful sexual desires in either the boy or the girl. So no breast touching and certainly no genital contact. Why? Because either so easily leads to the sexual desire itself rapidly outstripping the true language of relationship. Put more frankly, when a boy fondles a girl's breasts he generally finds that this gives him an erection and he wants an orgasm, and it requires a lot of self-control to stop at that: the next stage is likely to be mutual masturbation, and then intercourse. So physical passion has then turned love and gift into lust and use or abuse of one another. In marriage, when the two have become one through their mutual gift of each to the other, her joy is his and vice versa.

But surely times have changed and we live in a much freer world. For instance, is anything really wrong with masturbation?

The church recognises in her latest document on sex education that when teenage boys and girls start masturbating it is generally part of a growing up process which is almost inevitable, particularly with boys. But if we defend masturbation as an acceptable sexual act we must ask the question, what does it mean? If it communicates love it can only be communicating self-love. Is that what we want? For self-love tends to divide people, making it harder to share, to give, to love another. Especially when it is indulged as an end in itself.

But what about mutual masturbation. Surely that is sharing love?

Not really. It isolates an orgasm as an end in itself. Its object is not to be a physical expression of love and commitment but an isolated act of pleasure. It is generally used as a substitute for intercourse, and because it is concerned with the *use* of a body rather than the *gift* of a body it is seldom satisfying. Furthermore, masturbation weakens the will. People who habitually indulge in masturbation whenever they feel like it find that they have separated sex from love and that they will need sex in situations where there is no love. Such a condition makes fidelity and self-control in marriage hard to achieve.

But to allow no sexual contact before marriage seems impossible today.

Difficult, yes. Living in a society where the customs of behaviour and morals have drifted so far away from traditional Christian norms does put heavy pressure on young people to conform to what their social contemporaries expect of them, rather than the church. Hence they need a lot of understanding and support, rather than criticism and condemnation. But I wonder if the essentials have changed all that much. There is certainly far greater freedom in physical expression between the sexes, and far fewer safeguards. Young people go away together, share tents, bedrooms and flats without restraint, and in many ways have a more natural and relaxed relationship. But relationships are about becoming oneself, about loving and being loved, affirming and being affirmed, trusting and being trusted. I suggest that the blurring of the language, both verbal and bodily, has not provided more confidence in growth but rather less. Because a boy wants to undress you, or sleep with you, is it really because he loves you—as he will probably say—or because he hopes you will satisfy each other's sexual needs? And how can you tell the difference?

But does it matter as much as you suggest? O.K., we make mistakes but they are not the end of the world.

Does any lie matter? We are back, are we not, at the beginning.

What do you really want? If loving and being loved, trust and honesty, matter to you, then you will want such qualities in all your relationships, and that will mean no sexual intercourse before marriage. It will also mean careful, thoughtful and gentle use of physical intimacies in all relationships. After all, even if genital relationships and their preliminaries are reserved for committed and stable relationships, there remain plenty of happy, meaningful and true physical signs between boys and girls which express what they mean: hugging and holding bring so much—love, comfort, support, sympathy, joy, acceptance, affirmation, gratitude. Hugging can say virtually everything that needs to be said before marriage. And there is a real freedom in having made a decision not to have sex before marriage and then being able really to hug without the underlying, often unspoken question, as to what it might lead to.

Do you mean we can only hug each other before marriage? What about kissing? And surely it isn't either meaningless or excessively dangerous to fondle a girl's breast, especially if you love her very much?

Of course you must kiss each other. And you will know the difference between kisses that reflect love, tenderness and joy in each other's presence, and those that are hungry for sensation alone.

The problem about breast fondling is, quite simply, that it is never easy to stop there. It so easily stimulates sexual desire, especially in a boy, that he will want to go further. But it can, obviously, be a meaningful and loving moment, and one of real significance and sharing, when a girl lets a boy hold her breast. But only when it is significant, and not trivial, and it has to be recognised by both boy and girl that it is the furthermost intimacy that is or can be legitimately true of a relationship before marriage.

For when the body wants more than this it has stopped communicating what is true and merely wants physical satisfaction, even though it is obviously more agreeable to have sex with someone one is fond of. But this is the road to deceit, abuse of each other, uncertainty and guilt, no matter how well able one is to justify it afterwards and convince oneself that the relationship is wholly genuine. To promise everything with my body when not ready or able to acknowledge it in public through marriage is not being true to myself or my partner.

But what if you fail?

My teenage memories are of struggles in backs of cars, trying to get bras off girls. It took me a long time to learn the meaning of sexuality. But thirty years ago the fear of pregnancy and the social stigma it carried with it prevented much intercourse among young people. To-day, easy contraception and abortion, and society's rejection of Christian moral standards, have made it more necessary to learn those lessons more rapidly, and to be clear what you want and to stick to your principles. This is very difficult when one thinks again of the pressures put upon young people to conform, pressures from their own contemporaries, the media, and their own longings. Sticking to your principles will not lead to instant popularity but it will earn respect, particularly among your fellow Christians.

And if you do fail? Well, might I suggest that you don't be afraid of the sacrament of reconciliation, confession, as it is more commonly still called. God's forgiveness is real, complete and loving. The priest isn't going to despise you. On the contrary, he will respect and admire you for being honest, and it often helps to talk it over calmly, frankly and seriously with a priest. It is, after all, what he is there for. And honesty, with yourself, your boy or girl friend, the priest, and with God, does bring peace of soul and real happiness.

But I haven't really been to confession for years. I wouldn't know what to say.

One of the most common remarks made by Jesus in the gospels is that he came to call sinners. We sometimes forget that, besides being God, he also was truly a man, a human being like you and me. He was a teenager, a young man; the Epistle to the

Hebrews says that he 'was tempted in every way that we are'. He *understands* young people, he knows the longing, the desires, the pressures, the failures, the hopes. His longing is to be able to help: to offer healing, forgiveness, understanding and help.

Of course we are forgiven if we turn to him in our hearts. But the whole meaning of sacrament is that we experience the touch of God; and the sacrament of reconciliation is marvellously given to us to enable us to receive God's healing touch and to be helped by the pastoral support of the priest. What are priests for? To help Christians on their journey to God. To listen, advise, support, encourage; to be ever welcoming, understanding and supportive. When trying to live up to Christian values in this so-difficult and un-Christian world this sacrament is there precisely to help a young person do just that. No priest will condemn you for having failed in your sexual relationships. He only wants to help. Best, perhaps, if you haven't been to confession for ages, to go to a priest and ask for a chat and then tell him that you are nervous and don't know what to say.

And if you can't yet manage confession and are still unsure?

Then do not despair. If you are struggling for truth and honesty in all your relationships but still find that you are out of line with the church's guidelines, still unsure about so much, this does not mean that you are outside the church. You still belong, you are still loved, you are still part of the Body of Christ. But do not stop praying, trusting in God, and, if possible, do try to talk it all over with a priest.

VIII. Contraception

Why is the church so out of touch with the rest of the world about contraception?

Contrary to popular belief, the church does acknowledge and approve of birth control. She recognises the desirability of agreeing on the number of children a couple can cope with, more or less anyway, and she understands that there are many occasions when a couple really cannot manage another baby. The problem is what to do about it.

Some history may help here. Until fairly recent times child mortality was so high in this country, and elsewhere, that birth prevention was not a major problem. With the growth of improved medical care and the survival of the vast majority of babies the problem of over-large families became acute. And so the search for reliable methods of birth prevention grew apace. For many years the most common methods were either the male sheath, or the I.U.D., or various chemical creams, or withdrawal before ejacualation: none were outstandingly reliable. Then came the various types of pill and it seemed to many as if all women's troubles were over. But the church, believing that marriage is closely bound up with the procreation of children, and that any interference with the natural process of sexual intercourse is unlawful, came out firmly against any artificial methods of contraception, but did encourage the use of so-called natural methods, using the rhythms of the woman's menstrual cycle and restricting intercourse to those times when she was clearly not fertile.

One difference between artificial and natural methods is that the natural methods find out how the body works and harmonise sexual intercourse with the body rhythms, while the pill

'There are many occasions when a couple really cannot manage another baby'

changes the body rhythms by the use of chemicals. Temporary sterilisation by unnatural means is an interference with the natural life of the body. Furthermore, natural methods of birth control require co-operation of both husband and wife, often a shared self-control of postponement of pleasure.

Of course, much medical practice interferes with the natural life of the body, but its justification is that it is for a greater good. If a toe has gangrene it is justifiable to cut it off in order to save the life of the patient, but it is not so easy to justify sterilisation, temporary or otherwise, artificially induced, unless the reason is for a greater good. To prevent the birth of a child, preventing life rather than death, by such means needs considerable justification.

But as problems of population, such as over-crowding and health of mothers, came more into the public eye, more and more Catholics came to believe that *some* use of artificial methods of birth control was legitimate, for many found they could not use the natural methods and were in no condition to have more children. So Pope Paul VI set up a commission to advise him on the way ahead. In the event he more or less ignored the commission and produced his own encyclical letter, *Humanae Vitae*, an important and moving document, which emphasised the dignity of marriage and re-affirmed the church's condemnation of artificial methods of birth control. The encyclical upset many in the church, but most national hierarchies of bishops responded to the confusion by emphasising that, although the aim to be achieved was that of no use of artificial contraceptives, yet people who found themselves unable to avoid using them for what seemed to be the best of reasons should not consider themselves in grave sin and should continue to go to the sacraments and belong wholly to the church.

Pope John Paul II has repeated the strictures of the encyclical, but when he was in England in 1982 he spoke at York on the family and during his speech he specifically condemned what he called the 'contraceptive mentality', meaning that so much depends on motive. To *prefer* material luxury to children whether it is a second car, or a holiday in Spain, or just peace and quiet, would be examples of what he had in mind. If sexuality is entirely separated from creation of children, where does that leave marriage? What is the relationship then between marriage and sexuality? For children are *part* of a marriage, living signs of the parents' love and commitment to each other, and to envisage them as mere optional extras reduces marriage to a convenient way of life rather than as a sharing in God's way of learning how to love, which is how the church sees it. But there is more to it than that.

One of the effects of the easy availability of the contraceptive pill has been that men can now expect that women are always available for sex, whenever they are wanted. Does that sound crude? If it does, it is none the less the truth in many instances, both inside and outside marriage. The male expectancy tends to be that the girl will be on the pill (an expectancy encouraged, by the way, by most organisations claiming to give sexual advice to young people), or should be, if she had any sense, so that any pregnancy is certainly not *his* fault. This, together with the modern notion that sex is about performance, achieving orgasm, and has little or nothing to do with loving, commitment and giving, has meant that less and less of each other is now involved in sexual intercourse, even sometimes in marriage. Young husbands often *expect* their wives to go on the pill, without any discussion. And young women, without much question, do go on the pill. And no-one is keen to ask too many questions about the effects on women of many years of daily pill taking.

Some say, of course, that there would be even more abortions and unwanted babies if women did not use the pill, but that is assuming that the present day philosophy of sex as a shared pleasure, without responsibility or commitment, is correct. How beneficial has the pill really been? There is no doubt that it may have helped many married couples who have used it seriously and thoughtfully. But are families more stable, happier, more joyful? It seems doubtful. One in three marriages ends in divorce; there were 128,000 abortions in 1981; and the number of married women on tranquillisers and other drugs increases every year. The bookstalls are filled with magazines and paperbacks repeatedly emphasising the necessity of high class sexual performances if marriages are to succeed. Orgasm is the key, and if women don't experience it regularly something is wrong, with them or their husbands. Hence the anxiety, for sexuality in marriage has long ceased to be held as having much to do with growing in love, with expressing joy and healing and giving to one another, It is now considered widely to be about satisfactory performance, with the implication that someone who isn't a good sexual gymnast won't be much use as a married partner. Moreover, the modern practice of counselling young people to go on the pill at sixteen is a clear approval of sexual intercourse outside marriage and at the age when girls and boys are quite unable to sustain the commitment and responsibility required by a full sexual relationship.

A lot has happened in recent years to make natural methods of birth control more reliable and easier to use, although these developments have had little or no publicity. One of the main advantages of the natural methods is that they require both husband and wife to share in the decision and in the necessary self-control. They can each help with temperature taking, if required, and need to help and support one another at times when they cannot have intercourse. This need not weaken a relationship but, as many couples have testified, can truly strengthen it. A shared deprivation or pain can build up a relationship through the help and understanding each can give to the other.

The pill, on the other hand, is entirely the wife's responsibility and she has to bear all the possible side-effects, which are often not negligible. The whole issue is complicated, much more complicated than the media and the health authorities would have us believe. Early sexual intercourse is not good for adolescent girls, constant use of the pill is good for no women, yet the modern pressures on all girls to have sex means that both are happening. The use of contraceptives is closely bound up with our whole attitude to sexual intercourse and its meaning, part at least of what the Pope means when he condemns a 'contraceptive mentality'.

There is also the question of countries that are largely over-

'The bookstalls are filled with magazines and paperbacks repeatedly emphasising the necessity for high class sexual performances'

populated, but we in the West, constantly over-feeding ourselves and feeling guilty about the rest of the world, like to think that if the poorer Third World countries were to reduce their populations the problem of world hunger would be solved without much effort from us. Don't be taken in so easily. In the Third World children are a necessity to provide food and support for the families. If we in the first world were seriously to help the poorer countries to improve their standards of living by reliable methods of cultivation and distribution of food their need for large families would grow less. The peoples of many Third World countries, which are not Catholic, show little desire to have fewer children, for they need them and they love them.

Like so much else in this book the whole question needs more serious study, discussion, reflection and prayer. Above all a refusal to *assume* that the world's values are the best values. No young couple should marry without going into the question most thoroughly, if possible going on a Catholic Marriage Advisory Course or an Engaged Encounter Course. In this, as in all matters of sexuality, they should share their ideas and principles, hopes, beliefs and fears. The church helps with her guidelines and moral principles, and young people should respond by recognising that the church isn't simply out of date and the rest of society right. The church cares deeply about young people, about their happiness, their joy in marriage, their love for God and for each other. The whole question is too important and too precious to be dismissed summarily.

To young people who are on the pill, there is this to be said: it may help to look at the differences between what we call moral and pastoral theology. Moral theology lays down guidelines and tries to make clear in all areas of human behaviour the difference between right and wrong in the light of the gospel. Pastoral theology is concerned with what each person is capable of here and now, and starting, or re-starting, the journey to God from that point. For instance, moral theology says, quite rightly, that prostitution is wrong. But when a priest meets a prostitute who is longing to find God he doesn't say: 'cease your prostituting at once or you will never find God'. He will try to start from where she is—by helping her to start praying, reading a little of the Bible, coming to mass, thinking about other ways of earning a living. Then God may lead her to a position where she is able to change her way of life.

I don't want to compare a woman on the pill with a prostitute, but the principle is the same. The church's moral law teaches us that artificial means of contraception are not in harmony with God's law, so we call them disordered. But many a couple *cannot* at present do otherwise than use the pill. So the priest simply tries to help them grow towards God through prayer, reflection, living kindly and unselfishly. Maybe later, much later, they may be able to do things differently, maybe not. What is important pastorally is that they do not abandon their journey towards God.

IX. Prayer

Could you say something about prayer? I often try to pray but my thoughts wander and frequently, and sadly, it just seems to be a waste of time.

I sympathise. And anyone who has ever tried to pray will recognise your difficulties. But perhaps the first thing to say is that it is important not to think of prayer as some sort of achievement, a skill that can be learnt and improved upon. Prayer is about growing closer to God, it is part of the process of loving God more, of getting to know him better, of letting oneself be loved by him, of wanting to do his will, of offering oneself to God. We can learn a lot by thinking of how we get to know and love our fellow human beings. We need to listen to each other, to spend time together, to talk with each other about everything under the sun, to do things together, to touch one another, and some-

'We need to listen to each other, to spend time together'

times just to be with one another, especially when we truly love each other.

Of course, you cannot see or touch God physically, but there are advantages, too, when we are thinking about getting closer to God. One of the big problems about human love is the uncertainty about whether he or she loves me. How can I be sure? Now God has shown us the depths of his love by sending us his Son, Jesus, and giving him to us totally. Jesus' death on the cross for us is surely a sign that we can depend on God's love for us. In other words, the only uncertainty in my relationship with God is not his love for me but mine for him.

And yet one of the biggest questions is how we can be sure that God loves us and perhaps we need to ask him. Which raises the question of how do we communicate with God. I don't know how you pray at the moment but I expect you do most of the talking—either by reciting specific prayers or by talking to God in your own words, often no doubt asking him for things, sometimes thanking him, perhaps occasionally just sharing things with him. There is nothing wrong with any of these, indeed they are normal and excellent ways of praying, but a very important part of getting close to someone is to *listen* to them. To take time off and just listen to what they have to say. This is as true when we talk about getting closer to God. We need to give plenty of time to listening to him.

Obviously God doesn't speak in audible words that we can hear. But he does speak, sometimes in the silence of our own hearts, sometimes through the words of the scriptures, sometimes through things that happen to us, both good and bad, sometimes through the daily beauties of the world he has created. We need to learn how to look and listen with the eyes and ears of faith.

One way of starting is to get yourself very still and quiet so that you really can just listen to God in your heart. The important part is the silence and the stillness within yourself which aren't easy to reach, partly because we tend to be noisy and restless creatures, always wanting to be doing, thinking, imagining or talking. I'll tell you what I do and you may find it of some help.

First of all I get myself comfortable, usually by sitting down in an upright chair with my feet firmly on the ground (legs uncrossed) and my hands relaxed on my knees or in my lap. Some people prefer to kneel or to lie down but it is important to be comfortable and with a straight back if you are going to get yourself completely still. Then I take a little time to make sure that my body is relaxed and not stiff—that means deliberately relaxing my toes and fingers and shoulders which tend to get tense. Then I close my eyes (usually, though not always) and concentrate on listening to whatever sounds I can hear. Sometimes there is very little noise, especially when I pray in the early morning, but there may be creaks or movements or birds singing or the wind or footsteps or traffic sounds. My object is to concentrate so as to still my mind and sometimes it is quite hard work, needing fairly constant fresh starts as my mind has wandered. Then I become aware of my breathing and that is my entry, so to speak, to God. I reflect quietly that my breathing is the sign of life within me; that life is a gift from God; that God has promised to dwell within me, and that just by being alive I am truly close to God. And there I try to stay, occasionally bringing my mind and heart back to God as they stray away.

Sometimes it is hard to keep still, difficult to concentrate, impossible to remain at peace for more than a second or two. Then it is important to understand that prayer is an offering, that we bring to God what we are, and sometimes all we have to offer him is our restlessness and insecurity and perhaps depression. And we can give him a little of our time, which is not easy for anyone.

So I listen to God by trying to reach the stillness in my own heart. That means making a sort of journey down within myself. It needs a steady concentration, and an act of will, a desire to reach the quiet centre where God dwells. It also needs perseverance because it is easy to feel discouraged if no progress seems to be made. And yet, as I said earlier, prayer isn't a skill, it is a real longing to be with God, to listen to him, to grow closer to him, to want to learn how to love him. Some of the psalms provide helpful images of the sort of prayer I am

'First of all I get myself comfortable'

talking about: *'Be still and know that I am God'* (Ps. 45); *'As a weaned child on its mother's breast, even so is my soul'* (Ps. 130). Note that the child is weaned, not feeding but simply being held safely, trustingly, in its mother's arms.

Many of the men and women who have prayed deeply and have written about their experiences have suggested that the use of a phrase, or a line, or even a word steadily repeated, can help to keep the mind still and the heart firmly fixed on God. This is sometimes called a 'mantra' and it can be helpful. Taking a line of scripture, 'I will bless the Lord at all times'; or a phrase, 'My Lord and my God'; or the so-called Jesus prayer, 'Lord Jesus, Son of the living God, have mercy on me, a sinner', and quietly repeating it, perhaps in a rhythm of one's breathing, can produce a real stillness within.

There are many other ways of praying and some very good books on the subject. I can only suggest a few approaches, because each person must pray as they can, remembering that what we are talking about is a growing relationship, a growing friendship with God. It is a personal matter, you and God loving each other. Scripture can be a great help, perhaps especially the psalms. Try reading a passage slowly and gently and then you may find that it will lead you into a prayer of stillness. Then just stay there peacefully until your mind surfaces once again. Then read a little more.

Another way to read scripture is to take a passage from the gospels and to use your imagination as vividly as you can. Picture the scene in every small detail as if you were there with Jesus. Then listen carefully to what he is saying and reflect on how it relates to you; what is Jesus saying to you? We are all conscious of what we call the real presence of Jesus in holy communion, and sometimes we forget that Jesus is also truly present in the words of scripture, whether we listen to it being proclaimed at mass or whether we read it prayerfully to ourselves. Someone once described the scriptures as letters written by God to you and through them he does speak to you if you are ready to listen to him.

All these methods need time and silence and will: *wanting* to listen to God. If you live in a very noisy house I think it is important to try to make time and silence, even when circumstances are difficult. If you can there is much to be said for getting up earlier than the rest of the household, or going to bed later if you are not too tired. You don't need to start with long hours of prayer. If all you can manage is three really quiet minutes each day with God, then don't despise those minutes: they are precious and God will use them. Don't abandon the effort because you can't do much.

If silence at home is impossible to find then perhaps a short visit to a church or chapel, a library, or indeed a walk in the park. If you get accustomed to times of silence with God you will find it possible to pray in this way even when all around you are being noisy. You will be able to concentrate on the God who dwells in your heart and be with him no matter what is happening around you. For instance, when on a bus or a train, or in a waiting room or a queue, or in a church before mass.

The Bible tells us to pray at all times. That sounds impossible but really it is a matter of slowly growing closer to God, not just at specific times of prayer, but at all times. The more you pray the more you will want to pray. For instance, it is good to talk things over with God as you go about your daily routine. Think about things with him, things you have done, plans for the future, dreams and hopes; think also about your failures and disappointments. That may lead you to beginning to see God in the world around you, not only in the lovely things of nature—trees, blue sky, racing clouds, wind on your cheek, flowers, rain, hills and sea—but also in the tired eyes of people, the laughing eyes of children, the smiles of the people in the bus or in the shop, the welcome in the eyes of your friends; and also in the sad and tragic events of life, which often help us to see the guiding hand of God, always loving us, always wanting what is best for us.

Do not neglect formal prayers, either. They often help and at times very much so. They can provide a regularity, something to hold on to when life is difficult. When you cannot keep silent it is often helpful to say a prayer slowly and reflectively, the *'Our Father'* perhaps, or any other prayer you know and like. I frequently like to finish a time of prayer by saying the *'Glory be to the Father'* as an act of praise and thanksgiving. Many people, too, find the rosary one of the best of prayers.

The important part of the rosary is the reflection on the mysteries, quietly letting their meaning sink into your consciousness while peacefully saying the *'Hail Marys'* which keep your mind still. A constant meditation on those central mysteries of our faith is a very special way again of growing closer to God. Incidentally, you don't have to limit your rosary to the mysteries generally outlined in the prayer books. You could use the rosary to reflect on any of the mysteries of faith or any of the scenes from Our Lord's life as told in the gospels; the Last Supper, for instance, or the washing of the feet of the disciples, to name but two possibilities.

Remember, finally, that prayer is important, as important as spending time with anyone whom you want to love. If you do want to grow closer to God, to learn to love him, then I think prayer is crucially important. Don't, above all things, be discouraged if you find it difficult. God draws you to himself through your perseverance and your longing to find him. Sometimes you feel close to him and prayer is easy. At other times he seems miles away and prayer is a struggle and you may be tempted to abandon it as a waste of time. Please don't do that. It is by your fidelity to prayer in those bleak moments that you really grow in the love of God. Do not our human friendships and loves grow stronger when we are faithful to each other at difficult times? Your trust in God will grow if you persevere even when you don't feel like it. Prayer, above all, is letting God love you. Does anything matter more?

Nor is it childish to pray for things to happen or for people to get well. If you look at the gospels you will find Jesus constantly telling us to pray for what we need: to seek, to knock, to ask. God hears our prayers and responds to them. As someone has pointed out, he left a great deal of creation to be developed by the use of mankind's energies, intelligence, skills. Why not leave some things to our prayers? Never hesitate to ask God for what you want, for yourself and for others. He will answer your prayer, although not necessarily, of course, in literally the way you want. For he will give you what is best for you and that may involve failure or pain for a while. So pray with confidence and try to support your prayer with the prayer Jesus taught us: 'thy will be done'.

Some suggested books on prayer:
Prayers of Life by Michel Quoist (Gill and Macmillan).
To Grow in Christ—a plan for prayer by Damian Lundy (Kevin Mayhew).
Sadhana, a way to God by Anthony de Mello, SJ (Anand Press).
You: prayers for beginners and those who have forgotten how by Mark Link (Argus Communications).
Prayer and Contemplation by Robert Llewellyn (Fairacres Publications).